THE FACE OF SILENCE

THE FACE OF SILENCE

DHAN GOPAL MUKERJI

GYAN

Published by

GYAN

Gyan Publishing House
5, Ansari Road
Daryaganj, New Delhi-110002
Phone: 011-47034999, 9811692060
E-mail: books@gyanbooks.com

Distribution Network
gyanbooks.com
India, USA, Canada, UK, Australia

ISBN: 978-93-7316-431-1 (HB)

First Published, 1905

2nd Impression 2025

Printed at: Gyan Press, Delhi.

THE FACE OF SILENCE

Arthur: DHAN GOPAL MUKERJI

THE FACE OF SILENCE

BY

DHAN GOPAL MUKERJI

AUTHOR OF
"CASTE AND OUTCAST," "MY BROTHER'S FACE," ETC.

Dedicated

TO THOSE WHO POINTED ME THE PATH

JOSEPHINE MACLEOD

JADU GOPAL MUKHOPADHAYA

ALICE SPRAGUE

MRS. SUMNER HUNT

CONTENTS

THE FACE OF SILENCE

THE FACE OF SILENCE

CHAPTER I

RAMA KRISHNA MONASTERY

THAT a holy man, whom many of his followers called an Incarnation of God, lived in recent years near Calcutta, is one of the surprises of our time. Not only that. The most surprising thing about the matter is that I should go straight back from America, of the twentieth century, and find his followers leading their medieval life right in the center of modern progress. These monks and nuns living so close to the city of Calcutta, touching it at every vital point, yet maintained their aloofness from it with perfect ease. However, I must begin this story as it unfolded itself to me—bit by bit.

Through the kindness of a friend I had been invited to come and live in the Monastery where Rama Krishna's followers had their home. It looked quite imposing from the Calcutta side of the Ganges whence we approached it on a boat. The tower of a new temple stood out like a white nimbus above clumps of palm trees against the purple of the sunset sky. Below at its foot was a high stone palisade of graying yellow against which the river dragged its weary low tide. Soon our boat crossed the middle of the river. Now the rest of the monastery buildings raised their yellow heads one by one till the last little white shrine dedicated to the Divine Mother like a veil of silver came into view for a moment.

Suddenly they all vanished as we drew close to the embankment which rose like an immense precipice shutting everything from our view.

After we had moored our boat at the foot of the Ghaut we climbed its stairs in great haste. For we were afraid to be too late for Arati (even-song). On reaching the highest step we found ourselves on a large terrace of gray cement whence ran a small path toward the sacred shrine. Beyond the shrine gleamed the fierce green of the tropical gardens already taking on a softening tone of dull gold as the purple dusk stole down from the sky on wings of silence.

Just at that moment someone smote a gong in the shrine. That made us hasten within—for the Arati had begun. The shrine was divided into two rooms: inner and outer. We sat near a group of shaven-headed monks who occupied the scarlet floor of the outer shrine. They beat their several cymbals, and loudly chanted a benediction. While in the room beyond—the inner shrine—a monk in yellow waved a Pancha Pradip (a candelabrum of five lit candles) before a picture of Rama Krishna which occupied the flower-decked altar. And around the altar innumerable lamps—their wicks soaked in Ghrita (clarified butter)—lifted their fragrant flames to the image of the Teacher. Seen in that circle of light, Rama Krishna's picture afforded one the strangest impression: though he looked full of life yet he appeared inert as inertness itself.

"How came he to achieve that state?" I

pondered within myself, hoping to inquire into his career fully and critically later on. Just then the clashing of cymbals ceased along with the singing. The monk inside stopped waving the Pancha Pradip. After setting it down he took up a conch-shell and blew into it three times. After the last echo of that noise had died down he quietly seated himself before the altar and began to meditate. Following his example the Sanyasins (monks) in the outer shrine put away their cymbals; then chanted the thought on which they were to meditate. Now one by one they became still. Their bodies became rigid. Save their regular slow breathing which rose and fell in unison there was nothing to distinguish them from statues. Just then a sound like bees around a hive far away; the monk in the inner shrine chanted in a very low tone enunciating every word most clearly:

> "Whence our words come back broken, and thoughts return like dogs beaten in a chase, that silence over which gathers the dust of all sound. O river of Miracles. . . ."

That meditation like a sharp shearing current cut through my thoughts and flooded the entire room. Every face before me, each one of the monks, was austere like flint and as purged of desire as burnt gold. With eyes shut, mouths tightly closed, they went on fathoming that silence whose deeps "cannot be reached even by the plummets of stars!"

That was my first experience of the followers of Shree Rama Krishna. It fascinated me. And as I went on living with them I grew more and more curious to learn everything about their daily deeds. Why did they act as they did? What rules were they following in their conduct? Who formulated the scheme of their life? But the men whom I questioned said very little. They urged me "*to live* amongst them awhile longer."

The smoothness and simplicity that formed the routine of their life had a vivid reality under it. I could not avoid being conscious of the consecration that gave meaning even to their coming and going. Their faces shone with pure light. They were not troubled by false hopes, nor deluded by fancies. There was a grim but beautiful reality in all that they said and did. Every morning they rose before five in order to meditate for two hours. Then they went on to their day's deeds such as taking care of the sick, succoring the poor, and teaching the young.

At noon they held a short communion with the Lord, then had their dinner. A siesta followed. At about half past two they held classes in which erudite scholars discussed and taught Vedanta. The most illuminating interpretations of the Upanishads that I have ever known I heard in the class rooms of this monastery.

Then about four tea was served. At half past four all the monks went forth to take their favorite physical exercises. When evening came, as I have described, one met them in the shrine where the Arati was held.

These ocher-robed men walking across green lawns discoursing gently on God and Rama Krishna, were men of action as well. If there was sickness they looked after the sick of the neighboring locality. If there was famine in any part of India, or inundation, or plague they were there like an "eagle to its prey" to help the distressed. Once that was over they returned to the monastery to live and to be their own selves. Action never smirched them. Nor did inaction taint them with idleness. In one word they were free men.

And when I questioned them as to what had freed them from both pleasure and pain, they invariably pointed at the life and sayings of Shree Rama Krishna. "When all the sign-posts point to the same road," the proverb enjoins, "one is forced to take it." So when all the monks on each occasion pointed at the life of Rama Krishna I had to go and study it. "It is better to examine the source of the fountain," I was told.

But I did not go to a printed page. Early in my youth my mother had taught me: "Do not put a printed page between yourself and Life." So in order to study the life of Rama Krishna I began to look for its chroniclers and not the chronicle.

CHAPTER II

THE RAMA KRISHNA LEGEND

ONE morning I got a message from the Pundit. He was one of those disciples who had known Rama Krishna intimately. He had taken down many conversations of the Teacher. How he ever knew that I was searching for a man who had chronicled Rama Krishna's teachings I cannot tell. Anyway, the moment I received his kind invitation I went off to see him in his house.

The Pundit lived in the depths of the city on Amherst Street. When I reached the house I was surprised to find it so big. It was not beautiful, but large and clean. Its gray walls were pierced by tall windows with long bars of iron. In front of the house, railed off from the street, was a small playground. Now that I looked carefully I saw on the front gate a sign which said that this was a school building. But not to be deterred by any such bagatelle I opened the gate, crossed the playground, then pushed open the large green entrance door and entered the house. I was in the vestibule. Not a soul there, but I waited. In a short time a brown boy of ten or twelve, bare to the waist, came dashing down a stairway at the other end of the vestibule. I called out to him. The young monkey (as we would say endearingly) answered "My Lord, do you hunger to set eyes on our teacher, the Pundit?"

I said, "I am famine-stricken for him."

"Then follow me, O honorable," answered the lad. In a trice he was leading me up the stairs. That a lad of twelve could have the dignity of an elephant was proven to me by my young mentor. He walked so quickly yet so gracefully.

After climbing an almost endless series of steps I found myself on the third floor of the house face to face with a white-bearded man who was seated on a couch at an open window.

The little boy saluted him gravely, then said "The honored intruder craves to behold your blessed countenance." Then again saluting the Pundit gravely, he went out of the room as silently as sand shifts in an hour glass.

I felt so awed in the presence of the Pundit that I wished to do something as a token of my homage to him. So I knelt down, Brahmin though I was, and bowed to him, touching my forehead to the ground. At that instant I felt and heard a movement soft as a cat leaping. I looked up. There was the Pundit standing by me. Then he shouted in alarm, "What sacrilege! You, a Brahmin, prostrating yourself before a non-Brahmin!"

I scrambled up to my feet and rejoined, "But Rama Krishna has blessed you, which lifts you far above any Brahmin." Now I looked at him carefully. He was at least six feet tall; strong-chested like a gorilla. His face was that of a white-bearded tiger. He had strange brown eyes bordering on amber, and a magnificent Grecian nose with delicate almost effeminate nostrils; above that as if by sinister contrast rose his large brow and shaggy white mane that crowned his head with a sort of touseled halo. His height was all the more intensified by the long line of his snow-white robe falling in sheer straight lines down to his feet. He took me by the hand and seated me next to himself on the couch. He went on talking to me while my eyes wandered from wall to wall studying the room. It was the usual white-washed bare-walled affair—the beams showing from the ceiling like ribs of a famine-stricken man. Besides that couch on which we sat there was not another piece of furniture in the room. It was very hot that afternoon of May. Outside through the large iron-barred window one could see roofs of houses and a dusty metallic sky vibrating with heat. After having examined our setting I now paid full attention to my host. As he spoke I noticed in his words the tenderness which lay like a bloom on his voice. He was saying: "I have written down all that I heard the Guru Maharaj (Shree Rama Krishna) say. But the mouth from which these words dropped like stars from Heaven, how can I give you a sense of that? A mouth that was the cavern of Immortality!"

"Why do you say that?" I asked.

"If for no other reason," Puṇdit rejoined, "save this: whatever he said came true. His words of prophecy have all been fulfilled. No doubt Immortality lurked behind his thoughts. He was not erudite; nor did he speak with any dramatic force. He spoke as the common people speak, simply and directly. Yet his speech was not diseased with perishable qualities. They conveyed to his listeners the sharp tang of the imperishable. Though he is dead, his words keep on fulfilling their promise. Now let me ask you a question—you who bristle with a thousand questions. What do you wish to learn of Rama Krishna?"

"What do you mean, my Lord?" I begged.

"I mean, do you seek the Rama Krishna history, or the Rama Krishna legend?" The Pundit elucidated his question. Since I had not come prepared to answer a question like that, the Pundit had to wait till I thought the matter over. At last I was able to answer, "I seek just enough facts to enable me to gather all the trustworthy legends together."

"Good!" shouted my host with joy. His mane and beard seemed to tremble with pleasure. "Rama Krishna legends have not been gathered together. They contain more of the truth about him than all the authentic facts that I have written down. Legend is the chalice of truth. Facts are so veracious and so dull that nobody is uplifted by believing in them."

"But history is most necessary and most trustworthy," I exclaimed.

"Yes, it is necessary. Because on and around history will grow legend. As raw material for legend there is nothing finer than history. That is why I have written the Rama Krishna Chronicle. Five hundred years from now my work will find its fulfilment when a great poet will use it to create the Rama Krishna legend as deathless as my Master himself."

"Are there many Rama Krishna legends extant now?" I asked.

He shook his head and said "Yes, some. Go to Dakshineswar and all the surrounding villages. Call on their oldest inhabitants; then ask them questions. There are two old people living yet who saw him just at the time of his first illumination. They say that when he left the Kali Temple and passed by them, that day, there was such a light on his face that they could not bear to look at him. Go, visit those people. Whatever I know of the Holy One is committed to writing; it won't disappear tomorrow. But those old folks may die any time now. Listen to them, gather the music of their reed-flutes while they are yet able to pipe about the Lord."

"My Lord, is there anything else that I need to do while I go in search for the legends?" I pleaded for advice.

"Why should you do anything? Let the Lord who is within you speak out. Do not do anything. Only bear this in your mind: that you will hear nothing unusual or miraculous. Rama Krishna was the simplest of the simple. He said nothing to stir people to heroic deeds. Though eternity dwelt in his speech yet it did not put out such symbols of time as the sun and the moon. He did not do anything that can be of theatrical interest to a story-teller, though his touch revealed God to many men."

"His touch revealed God to men!" I exclaimed in amazement.

The Pundit answered gravely, "Whenever he spoke of God a light unknown on earth would come on his face; then if he touched anyone with his hand or foot that person would see the whole world bathed in radiance, and Ananda (Bliss) for at least three to four days. He would behold all faces bright as the stars, all places bright as if they had put on the full moon for a dress, and all the dark spaces of the night would be as vivid as the morning sun. In those six days that I was illumined, life was one. There was no death. Day and night were not marked by any difference: Anandarupa—the light of bliss—shone on all hours and all things. And the heart of all existence sang but one song: 'Words cannot speak of this *Abam Manasogocharam* and the mind cannot come near it. I am the Light of Silence eternal. I am Bliss, I am Bliss!'" The Pundit stopped. The memory of his first spiritual experience filled his face with radiance. His eyes were filled with tears that shone like gems. Words and questions that had occupied my mind now fled as dogs before a tiger. I took the dust from the Pundit's feet. Then I rose to go in search of those other men and women who had seen and known Rama Krishna, in order to gather from their living lips the story of his life.

CHAPTER III

RAMA KRISHNA'S EARLY LIFE

ACCORDING to the legends Rama Krishna was born in the spring of 1836, in the famous Chattapadhaya family of the Brahmins of Bengal. At birth he was named Gadadhar which was later abbreviated into Gadai Chattujjay.

His parents gave him the usual education of a Brahmin boy of the 'forties of the last century. It consisted of studying in Sanskrit such books as the Gita, the Ramayana and the Mahabharata, besides a thorough training in meditation. Though he showed an exceptional aptitude in learning meditation, Rama Krishna proved himself but of average intelligence when it came to studying philosophical works. He could not stomach any metaphysics. On the contrary he loved books on sacred matters so that he devoured hundreds of ballads and poems that dealt with the lives of the saints and gods of Hinduism. In fact there was no one else of his age who could recite from memory such a volume of religious poetry and lore of mysticism.

Since he was so earnestly devoted to matters of religion his family decided to dedicate him to the priesthood. And before he was sixteen years old he was made an acolyte in the Kali Temple of Rani (Queen) Rash Mani who, though a woman, was one of the most able rulers that feudal India has known. It was her spiritual acumen that directed her two sons-in-law to appoint Rama Krishna her family chaplain by the time he was eighteen years old.

The legend has it that the Rani and her entire household became aware of their young priest's spiritual powers from the very first day he came to their temple. And during her lifetime as well as that of her sons-in-law they guarded and cherished him with the utmost care and appreciation. Even at the present time nearly forty years after his death in that village (Dakshineswar) one is told tales of the friendship that Queen Rash Mani's household showed to him the very day Rama Krishna came there as an acolyte.

No doubt from the very start the kindness of the royal household made Rama Krishna feel at home in Dakshineswar. The place itself was very beautiful and spacious. The temple stood in the heart of a garden which spread for acres along the shore of the Ganges. Hundreds of boats, red, blue, white and green drifted by towards Calcutta which was only six miles down the river. Even now when the temple grounds have fallen into neglect, one feels the majesty of the place. The gray turrets and domes of the shrines, the palatial halls and corridors, and the long dark inmost sanctuary lit by scores of torches where the white-vestured priests are seated meditating on Silence, give one the feeling of nostalgia for the Unknown. Outside in the garden the plants, grasses and weeds gleam like flames of emerald under the fierce Indian sun. Then if one looks further to the north, one sees the forest of Panchabati whose immense trees with their far-spreading branches afforded Rama Krishna the necessary solitude for his meditations.

All the stories that one hears about him make it abundantly clear that in his impregnable isolation of Panchabati, Rama Krishna not only had his most vital spiritual experience, but he went thither from the very first to find relief from the strenuous and intricate task of administering a royal chapel. He did it with greater frequency as his work at the Kali temple defined itself more and more clearly. The potential holy man in him realised that he was expected to be a prince of the church. Suddenly he said to himself, "This temple is too rich. Its income is fabulous. It wears out the soul of the ministrant priest. It gives him no time to meditate on God."

In other words Rama Krishna came from a simple, poor, and very religious Brahmin home in the country to take care of a famous palace of worship as if he had been a mighty potentate of the medieval church. What was expected of him by the people of the surrounding countryside was not holiness and mysticism, but elegance, dignity, and spiritual diplomacy. "They expected him to flatter the rich and feed the poor," says one of his younger contemporaries. "But, alas!" continues the same contemporary, "they counted without the mystical nature of their priest and the symbolism of the goddess whom he worshipped. It is certain that Kali, the symbol of Time and Eternity, of Death and Immortality, made so deep an impression on the young Rama Krishna that he had no illusion nor desire to become a prince among priests.

"That grim image whom he worshipped daily, drew forth from his soul the man that he really was—a mystic, and not a theologian. He devoted more time to prayers and meditation than was prescribed by the usual observances of the priesthood. He paid a minimum of attention to rituals by insisting that in the inner shrine stood the Goddess Kali not as a dead fact but as a living symbol of man's spiritual experience."

The symbolism of Kali means Time, and Akalé, Beyond Time, Immortality! She is the Mother of the Universe as well as its destroyer. Out of Her all things come, and into Her all return. Her image, which is that of a dancer, is hewn out of black marble, for Time is invisible: it has no color. And yet because we experience ceaselessly the succession of Time's moments the symbol of Time lies in the art of dancing which is a succession of movements. Moments of time are but movements of men. When man sees with his eyes he beholds only space, but when he dances he experiences Time. Hence Kali, the symbol of our experience of Time must needs be an image of the dance. And she must also wear a garland of human heads around her neck, for those are the epochs of man's life-history that time wipes out of existence. Beside those weird ornaments she has four hands which are emblems of the three features of time: the past, the present and the future. The first two hands, holding a sword and a human head each, mean: that man, the latest embodiment of human destiny, is being wiped out by death. Her other two hands are raised to indicate hope (the future) and memory (the past). Such is Kali. But that is not all, for behold, Kali is stepping on Shiva, the snow-white god under her foot: he is the symbol of Immortality, for he is the god of renunciation, whom she cannot vanquish. Suddenly the frenzied movements of her dance are arrested, for Shiva is unconquerable. She who has conquered all cannot conquer the God of Renunciation. Hindus understand Kali perfectly. Even children learn to pray to her thus:

> Show me thy face of compassion which has been hidden by the dust of illusion. O Goddess, thou face of Immortality, reach me through and through with thy deathless Compassionateness.

The stark clarity of the symbolism of Kali, that nothing abides but Renunciation, made Rama Krishna see through the pageantry of rituals and rites. How could he see the meaning of Her Presence and yet remain a prince of the church? Though not yet out of his teens he understood her message and set out to shape his sacerdotal duties accordingly. First of all he gave up his silken vestments and gold-embroidered silver chudders. He refused to eat from plates of gold, waited on by a dozen servants. Last of all he moved from his sumptuously furnished residence into the little room near the servants' quarters where he lived for the rest of his life. Having done that he set out to simplify some of the most ornamental services of the temple. No more did he put on himself the ceremonial garlands of pearls, dhoti, the vestment of scarlet silk, the chudder of gossamer blue shot with bits of diamonds like stars. He refused to wave censers of gold before his deity, and gave up reading to the people from a book held between gold-embossed covers. As he whittled down the intricate pictorial rituals he concentrated more and more on learning and teaching his congregation the inner meaning of their worship.

Of course the visitors to the temple began to complain of his iconoclasm. They appealed to Queen Rash Mani to have the young priest summarily discharged. But she said to them, "Why should we dismiss him because he worships Kali in his own way; he is a priest, he ought to know what is proper better than we do. As long as he wears the garb of industriousness, as long as purity dwells in his speech, and morality in his deeds, it is idle to criticize him."

Hardly had that deputation returned home when another made up of the most respectable people of the outer neighborhood waited on the Rani. They complained, "O Rani, Mirror of Truth and Protector of Religion, please dismiss your priest Godai Chattujay for he seems to be somewhat mad."

This time the "Mirror of Truth" answered: "He is not insane. He is afflicted with the superior madness of a saint."

Now for the space of a year or so Rama Krishna was left alone, though he acted as strangely as he pleased. He soon formed the habit of praying to the Goddess Kali at unusual hours. At night or during the afternoon siesta when the doors of the inner shrine were shut and when the deity was supposed to take her rest, one could hear the young priest crying and praying within: "O Mother, give me wisdom. Make me see your loving Face that you hide under that mask of stone."

At last the frenzy of his praying began to annoy the respectable people of Dakshineswar again. But instead of complaining to the Rani they grumbled amongst themselves. They said "This is outrageous. There is a time for sleeping and a time for praying. No respectable priest disturbs his deity with talk when he should be asleep in bed. He acts more and more fantastically! What are we to do?"

Hriday, a nephew of Rama Krishna's, who was his constant companion, tells some very revealing stories about the Master's eccentricities. First of all, though a Brahmin of the Brahmins, yet because the golden rule of Hinduism says that one must see God in everyone, Rama Krishna used to eat what was left over from the plates of the outcast beggars that dined at Dakshineswar. This was violating the caste rules in which he had been brought up and which all Hindus accept. Yet the most orthodox people about the place willingly shut their eyes to his strange conduct. Another day when he was offering rice and sweets, the liturgic offerings, to Kali, a cat crept into the shrine and mewed for food. Rama Krishna instantly turned to the wretched animal and fed it, saying, "Ah, Mother, you have come disguised as an animal; since you are in all beings, I offer it to you. Eat, stop your mewing."

No doubt all these incidents show that Rama Krishna after a time compelled acquiescence if not respect from all the people. And they also verify his consistent standard of living: he put into practice what religion teaches.

But what people saw him do in public was nothing compared with what he strove for in private, which is illustrated by the story of his overcoming the desire for wealth. He prayed to Kali to give him the right conception of money. He did not rest with praying. He constantly meditated on the following sentence from the scriptures: "Gold is clay; clay is Gold." Sometimes to prove it in conduct, he gave away the gold and silver offerings that were brought to him by rich pilgrims. Thus he prayed and practised for nearly a year, yet reached no solution of the problem of money. He prayed and meditated for hours every day. As he says himself, "I was most deeply perplexed by the problem of money. Our religion teaches that gold and dust are one. Since I took my religion seriously, month after month every morning, I held a coin and a little clay together in my hand and meditated, 'Gold is clay and clay is gold,' yet that produced no spiritual experience in me. Nothing proved the truth of that statement. I do not remember after how many months' meditation, one day I was sitting on the river bank very early in the morning. I prayed to the Mother to give me light. Lo! suddenly I beheld the whole world in the radiant vesture of gold. Then it changed into a deeper luster—the color of brown clay more beautiful than gold. With that vision deep down in my soul I heard like the trumpeting of ten thousand elephants: 'Clay and gold are One to Thee.' Now that my prayers were answered I flung both gold and clay into the Ganges."

From that day Rama Krishna lived unafraid of money, or the lack of it. His attitude toward it was perfectly balanced. He never said such shallow things as, "Lucre is filthy"; nor did he say "Money is power." As with wealth so with every other of life's problems he held, and later taught his disciples that one must rise above the "opposites"—two aspects of the same thing. He used to say to his disciples "To neglect money, or not to give any account of it, is just as erroneous as to hoard it like a miser. Money buys a few things, that is true; but the ladder to Heaven is not made of gold." There is a story current in India that one day one of his young apostles went shopping. He considered bargaining with the shop-keepers too materialistic, hence beneath his dignity. So he made his purchases and returned to Dakshineswar. Then when he opened his bag and showed Rama Krishna the small size of the goods he had bought, the Master wanted to know why he had paid so much for so little. The young holy man answered "I did not drive any bargain." Then he gave his reason for it. "I did not drive a bargain, my Lord, for that is not spiritual." But Rama Krishna answered

"What, you think because you neglect to learn the art of bargaining, God will make you a holy man? Fie! A holy man is he who has contempt for nothing. While in the bazaar of life you must learn to master its laws. Do not confuse holiness with idiocy. Your spiritual life makes you most compassionate. It also makes you infinitely more vigilant than those who live in the world. Brahma, God, is Bliss Infinite, no doubt; but He is also Infinite Intelligence!"

Though the pleasure of recounting such incidents as the above is very great, we must resist that temptation and ask the reader to go back to the Kali temple where we left Rama Krishna practising the religious austerities of his teens. We have already noticed that so much religious earnestness in one so young appeared utterly eccentric, if not mad.

At last he did something that proved to the worldly that he was too insane to be a priest; he flagrantly neglected his duties at the temple. Sometimes he secluded himself for days at a stretch in the woods of Panchabati. Were it not for his nephew Hriday who acted as his substitute, the business of Kali-worship would have collapsed. This happened nearly a dozen times. Now all the people of Dakshineswar with the exception of the Rani's household were convinced beyond any doubt that their priest had truly gone mad. A very large deputation waited on the Rani. They demanded that he be sent away. But again Rash Mani refused to act according to their request. She answered "I am certain he is the coming Teacher. We must be patient with this Lion-cub of spirituality for treating our temple as his native desert."

Those words of Rash Mani's convinced everyone that they must expect nothing from the Rani save more advice to endure Rama Krishna's eccentric actions. Instead of being vindictive, the people of the countryside felt so sorry for Rama Krishna that some of them traveled a hundred miles into the interior in order to break the melancholy news to his mother. She was told "God has cracked your son's mind." But that wise lady was not perturbed by the news, though she was a little puzzled. So in order to see him with her own eyes she came to Dakshineswar. One look at him convinced her that he was far from mad. Just the same she was afraid that he would give up the world and take the vow of celibacy, and a monastery was the last place where she wished to see him. In order to prevent his becoming a monk she urged him to marry. "Marriage," everybody counseled, "will put an end to all this God-madness." The time-worn threadbare Indian method of keeping a man from going mad about the Infinite, has been to wed him swiftly to a young woman. This stratagem was tried on Buddha too. Though it never succeeds in bringing about the desired end, parents take to it as a hangman to the noose.

However, after a time Rama Krishna announced to his mother that he was quite willing to marry a young girl whom the Divine Mother had shown to him in his meditations. They followed his directions as he gave them. About four hundred miles away the bride dwelt with her parents. There, to the amazement of the matchmakers, they found the eligible Brahmin girl as Rama Krishna had said. Her name was Sarada—the world's desire. In proper time and place Rama Krishna was married to her.

He brought his wife home to Dakshineswar. Then he did a thing that a saint addicted to superior madness would do. He said to her, "Do you see that tower? It is big and spacious. You will find everything there that you need. Go, and meditate and pray to God to give me illumination. Why should you do it?—because it takes two women to make a man holy—his mother and his wife. My mother has brought me thus far, now it is your task to be my other mother, not my wife, and to take me across the river of delusion to the House of Heaven." The little wife did as she was told. She went and lived in that tower. It was high, and its windows gave on to the Ganges to the west, to the gardens and the temple in the east. North and south of that tower were tall trees. To that seclusion she banished herself. With the exception of her girl friends she saw no one. Her husband she saw rarely except during those hours when he performed the common rites of the Temple. Those were very hard years for her. No less hard for him, for he was meditating and praying day and night. The legend runs that he never slept during this period.

He was pressing closer and closer to the ultimate mystery. Like a true Hindu wife she was glad and proud to help him walk the path of renunciation and holiness. Yet her own life was not full enough. And she suffered moments of loneliness. It was during one of those moments that she came to Rama Krishna and said: "My Lord, I want children." Rama Krishna answered "Your children will be many, and they shall come from the ends of the earth. I already see them coming to you, though some of them speak languages that you do not know!" The ring of authority was so great in his voice that the "holy mother" bowed before it. She went back to her life of prayers and devotion in that tower.

About fifty years later when some English and American devotees came to pay their homage to the "holy mother" (as she is called in India) she said aloud: "His words have come true. I have children, whose language I do not understand."

CHAPTER IV

HOLY MAN

AT last when he was about thirty years old, Rama Krishna had his first Illumination. It came to him early one morning. After he had finished the morning rites of the temple, he sat down before Kali and said to her: "Mother, either I receive illumination to-day, or I shall take my life to-morrow. I have prayed and meditated a dozen years now. I have practised all the austerities prescribed by each and every teacher that came my way. I have lived according to the teachings of our holy books that you have revealed to men. Yet, Mother, you do not grant me the Vision of your Face. If you do not show it to me to-morrow I will take this life that you have given me."

Then he sat still and meditated. "Those

who with steadfast love seek Me shall find Me," says the Lord in the Gita. Rama Krishna repeated that line to himself with the most fervent sincerity. And whenever his mind tired of repeating it he prayed: "Break my heart, Mother, but end my doubts. Show me your Face of Immortality."

Suddenly her arms of stone moved. Her lips changed into two burning petals of Light. Thence the Light spread all over her face. Now her hair caught fire and glowed like a circle of infinite flame, as if the very sun had come down from Heaven and stood behind her. Now the Light danced and coursed down her body, down, down to the Shiva lying under her feet, but it did not stop there. Like eagle-wings the conflagration spread over the whole shrine in an instant. Even small things like the bells, the candles and the flowers danced, possessed by the unearthly radiance.

Wherever Rama Krishna looked, he saw Light, Light, Light.

"I have found you, I have found you." Crying, he dashed out of the temple. Wherever he went he saw nothing but light. The Ganges curved at his feet like a sickle of gold. The shore on which he stood was but a rock of solid flame. The trees in the distance, the boats and their boatmen in the middle of the river, the birds coursing through the sky, and the very sky itself sang possessed of the Divine Light. "I have found you, I have found you!" He cried with the Rishis of old:

> "Harken unto me, ye sons of Immortality. I have found Him the Person Supreme! Even the Gods—those dwellers in the highest spaces—are humbled now that I have found Him the sun-clad One!"

According to some observers Rama Krishna stayed in that state of ecstasy for nearly two weeks, while others testify that he had the experience only for a few days. But they all agree that during that time he neither ate nor drank. He praised God continually. He said to one and all "I see the Divine Mother in you. Can't you see Her? There She is in your eyes, in your voice, in your heart—the fathomless river of Bliss." Sometimes as he spoke the light that shone on his face would become so bright that people had to hide their eyes lest they be blinded.

As everyone knows, news spreads very rapidly in the East. Within a fortnight of his attaining Illumination, scores and hundreds of people came to Dakshineswar to see the Holy Man. Though Rani Rash Mani had been dead many years now, yet her sons-in-law who had stood by Rama Krishna felt blessed at the fulfillment of his search, and, ready to serve him to the best of their ability, extended their hospitality to all who journeyed to their Kali Temple. No matter how large the number of pilgrims, they were all fed and given shelter in the royal mansion. "You are welcome," they were told. "Do not thank us. We but seek to acquire merit by serving our Holy Man."

Weeks passed into months, bringing in their train many more pilgrims. Rama Krishna instructed and blessed each one in the Name of the Mother. He ceased to avoid people. On the contrary he welcomed them now. He put an abrupt end to all his so-called eccentricities. He stopped praying to Kali during forbidden hours, and performed all his priestly duties at the temple with the regularity of a clock. Even the most intricate rituals could no longer tax his patience. Now he lived under the public gaze without ever running away to the seclusion of the Panchabati woods.

Eye-witnesses say that at this time such a power emanated from him that no one could pass by without stopping to salute him. Whether in the streets or in the temple people were bound to stand still a moment if their eyes fell on Rama Krishna. "Though he compelled attention, yet his face bore no expression but one of humility." And the strange attraction that emanated from him never ceased.

Soon he began to attract people from remoter parts of India. Flocks of pilgrims came to obtain Darasana (Vision of his face). "For," they reasoned, "a sight of the face of an illumined soul washes away the sins of a life-time."

Of course none of them knew the exact nature of Rama Krishna's recent experience. It is doubtful if he himself had realised fully the limits thereof. He was full of Ananda, bliss; he cared for nothing else.

One morning a very strange man came to see him. He was of the West country, and judged by his appearance the man was an advanced Teacher. But since Rama Krishna was busy performing the rites of the temple, the newcomer had to wait till the afternoon, when he joined the group of pilgrims who had come to be instructed by the young Master.

It was nearly ten in the evening when the assembled multitude dispersed, leaving Rama Krishna alone to meditate on the river bank. Now Totapuri, for that was the Teacher's name, approached him.

Rama Krishna said to him, "Why have you not gone away with the other pilgrims? If you want a bed here, the royal mansion will accommodate you for the night."

The Teacher answered, "I have not come to beg for hospitality. I want speech with thee. My friend, thy soul has climbed the first flight of stairs that lead to the House of Silence. There are two more flights to mount."

Rama Krishna not at all surprised said, "What are they?"

The Teacher propounded: "Thou knowest the story of Rama and Hanuman. When that incarnation of God said to Hanuman, 'How dost thou perceive me, O my beloved devotee?' —what did Hanuman answer?"

"Hanuman said," replied Rama Krishna, " 'When I feel you, my Lord, I am your son and servant. When I think you, I am a part of you. But when I realised you—I am you.' "

"You have felt your Mother. Now it is for you to think and realise Her. Do you not wish to attain Oneness with God?"

"What will happen to me if I attain Oneness?" asked Rama Krishna.

The Teacher said, "Then all this Thou-and-Me conception of God will come to an end. You will lose your self—your Me-ness."

Rama Krishna smiled with mischief. "But I can lose my Me-ness by going to sleep, or, through a fainting fit."

The Teacher who was apparently without a sense of humour retorted: "But that is not Samadhi (Oneness). In sleep or in a fainting fit the Me-ness remains though it is not articulate. The instrument, the brain, through which it articulates itself is disturbed. That is all. All the desires and passions are present as the food is present in the recently dined well-fed man, who has suspended digestion for some moments. When a man is asleep or lying in a swoon his heart goes on beating. The pulse does not stop, nor does the circulation of the blood. These are signs and symbols of Me-ness. In Samadhi all these functions of man stop. The other signs of Me-ness in sleep are just as interesting in their total difference from those of Samadhi. A man recovering from a sudden loss of consciousness or coming out of sleep is the same man filled with the same desires, passions and ambitions, that he took with himself to bed. He is no better coming out of an unconscious state than when he went in."

Rama Krishna interrupted: "But what would I gain by attaining Oneness?"

The Teacher answered: "A man who enters that state is bound to lose all his Me-ness—its petty desires, lusts, hopes and weaknesses. When he emerges from it he is a bridge to Immortality! He is filled with joy, compassion, and discrimination. While in Samadhi, though his heart and pulse do not beat, yet he is not dead. In fact his life is keen as the sharpness of a razor. His experiences have grown sharper and more inclusive. For all the worlds—matter, mind, and the spirit—live in him. Within him all the experiences of Reality find their nest. He becomes That (Tat) in which all beings find their homing place. After he has had Samadhi, a man feels himself not a part but all of God. He has become the backbone of the universe, nay, the very measurement of Immortality!"

The Teacher spoke those last words with great conviction. It moved Rama Krishna. But he was very cautious. He asked "What do you wish me to do?"

The Teacher said: "I would have you learn higher meditation. You are an advanced seeker. I will initiate you into Advaita Vedanta—the science of attaining Identity."

"But," objected Rama Krishna, "I cannot do anything without the Divine Mother's consent."

The Teacher paused a few moments, then said cryptically: "Then go and get it from Her."

Rama Krishna went away silently while Totapuri sat on the river bank and meditated.

In the meantime, inside the shrine, Rama Krishna communed with Kali. After an hour or so he heard her command: "Yes, my son, go and learn of him."

He returned and said to Totapuri that he had obtained the Mother's permission. The Teacher, though struck by the innocent simplicity of the young man, perhaps smiled at his apparent superstition in addressing the image in the temple as Mother. A great Vedantin, he did not believe in a personal God, nor did he believe in the efficacy of prayer, or devotion to a Creator. But he said nothing to Rama Krishna on that point, thinking that under his training the disciple would know the truth and spontaneously brush aside his superstitions.

Later on, the Teacher informed Rama Krishna that he must be initiated with proper ceremony into the secret mysteries before beginning to learn the truths of Vedanta or practising its disciplines. He must give up the insignia of his present state of life, such as the sacred thread and tonsor which marked him as a Brahmin. He must begin a new life. Rama Krishna agreed.

Totapuri then went to the deepest part of the woods of Panchabati and took up his residence there. Every day for some hours Rama Krishna came to receive his preliminary instructions. And as soon as that was over, the Teacher set the date for Initiation. Again Rama Krishna went into the Kali Temple and communed with the Mother. And again She commanded him to follow his teacher and attain Oneness.

At last on the auspicious day, Rama Krishna renounced his position as the priest of the temple and went forth into the woods of Panchabati.

On the altar that Totapuri had already built, they lit the sandal-wood fire.

Now Rama Krishna was ordered to perform his own funeral ceremony. One must cremate all of the finite consciousness in thought and speech before one can be taught Advaita, the science of Identity. So there he stood in the dense forest facing his Guru across the altar. He chanted, "I renounce my father, my mother, and my wife. I renounce my learning and my knowledge. I renounce my name and my station. I renounce my feelings, and I renounce my thoughts. O fire, thou symbol of immortal purity. O ye trees, the very emblem of all Life, O thou sky, thou witness of God's silence—witness with my Guru that into this burning pyre I fling my earthliness and my Me-ness! I proclaim my Self homeless in Time. I proclaim my Self homeless in space. And I proclaim my Self homeless in the heavens. I proclaim my Self homeless in all save Him, the God Eternal, Infinite, and Silent. Burn me, O Fire, till I am no more."

Totapuri took him by the hand and

walked around the fire seven times. Now Rama Krishna flung into it all the insignia and symbols of his caste and station. Then he meditated a long while, facing the fire. He was asked to renounce his name, Gadadhar Chattapadhaya, that his parents had given him. That too he renounced.

Totapuri took him by the hand again and led him into a small hut. There he and Rama Krishna sat down to meditate on "I am God. I am Infinite Bliss. I am Infinite Knowledge. I have no name, nor form. I am One! I am He."

Hour after hour passed. The day turned into night, yet those two meditated. The moon rose higher and higher. The night declined. The sun rose again. Yet the two holy men went on meditating.

When the sun had set the second time and the moon had risen again, suddenly Rama Krishna shouted, "I cannot go beyond this point." The Teacher asked, "Why can you not?"

The disciple cried out: "I see The Mother

before me. I want to worship Her as Her servant. I do not wish to attain Identity."

"Why this weakness? Are you to remain a child for ever? Begin again."

Again they chanted the Mantram of Oneness and plunged into meditation. Regarding his second attempt Rama Krishna later told his own disciples: "I failed to bring my mind to the Brahman—Absolute. I had no difficulty in withdrawing the mind from all earthly objects, but I could not obliterate from my consciousness the all too familar form of the Blissful Mother who appeared before me as a living reality and would not allow me to pass beyond. She was all name and form! Again and again I tried to concentrate my mind upon the Brahman, but every time The Mother's form stood in my way. In despair I said again to the Guru 'It is hopeless. I cannot raise my mind to the unconditioned state and come face to face with my Self—the Absolute.' The Teacher said sharply, 'What! You cannot do it? But you must.' He cast his eyes about the dimly lighted room and finding in a corner a piece of broken glass he took it up and pressing its point between my eyebrows said, 'Concentrate thy mind on this point!' Then with a stern determination I again set to meditate. I felt an appalling pain between my eyes, and in the heart of that agony danced like a flame, the gracious form of the Mother! I used my discrimination now. As a sword cuts to pieces a body, so with my discrimination I severed her into two. Nothing obstructed me now. I at once soared beyond name and form, above pain and pleasure, and I found myself at One with the Absolute. Before that supreme ecstasy the senses and the mind stopped their functions. The body became motionless like a corpse. The universe rolled away from my vision—even space itself melted away. Everything was reduced to ideas which floated like shadows on the dim silence of the mind. Only the faint consciousness of 'I, I,' repeated itself in dull monotony. My soul became the Self of Reality, and all idea of dualism of subject and object was gone. My Self knew no bounds. All life was one Infinite Bliss! Beyond speech, beyond articulate experience and beyond thought! To call that state even freedom is to limit its meaning."

From that day on Totapuri called him Rama Krishna Paramhamsa—the Lord and Master Supreme. Following his example, all India now calls him by that name. In a few weeks after that great event Totapuri went away as he had come, unknown and unseen by the multitudes. He had fulfilled his task. But Rama Krishna always voiced his gratitude to him whom he called "Nangta" (the unclad one).

It was about this time that people saw his appearance alter. First the expression of his face changed. It grew to look like a mask, save his eyes where dwelt a new light deeply tranquil "but fierce with love." And by contrast with the expression of his "young eyes" the rest of his face looked all the more aged. People said, "He has ceased to live in his face; now you can see in his eyes that he lives only in his Soul." Not only his face but also his strong athletic body, so agile and quick, now clung to him like a blanket—something that he washed and cleansed, and carried about. That is exactly what one feels when one looks at the photographs of Rama Krishna in the shrine of the monastery.

From now on he had two distinct appearances, one inner and the other outer. "Physically," says Saradananda, "he was unconscious of earthly matters: half the time he was unaware whether he wore anything or not. His disciples saw to it that his clothes were all on him. Though he bathed and cleansed his body regularly, yet to an outsider he looked like a man utterly careless about it." He was so detached from it that it was not even a burden to him. He dwelt in it as a log floats on the tide. Better still—he lived in his body as the fire abides in the wood. Yet whenever he spoke of the Lord, its very pores grew radiant. "Holiness exuded from him as fragrance from flowers."

"Neither you," said another who knew Rama Krishna, "nor any other man who never saw him and heard his words can conceive by looking at any of his photographs the Flame that he was. In a photograph you see only his ashes, not that conflagration of spirituality that is spreading from soul to soul throughout Hindusthan. Even if you saw him sitting still at ease he would look as inert as that picture. But if you took the name of God in his presence then he would lose his body. You express surprise? But how else can I put it? If you can imagine a man wrapped in raiments of ecstasy, of such luster that he was all Light and no flesh, then you have truly beheld him. Yes, sometimes he became so radiant that all of us had to hide our faces before his Presence. It appears peculiar to those who know not the ways of God-consciousness. But it is quite natural that the mere taking the name of God may inspire a soul to spiritual ecstasy. Rama Krishna could be kindled even by a chance word, the sight of a face, the shifting of the tide of the Ganges, and many such common everyday occurrences."

At this time his attitude towards his wife changed. Now he requested her to come out of her secluded tower and live near him. From that time she looked after him and his disciples. This was not an easy task. She had to keep house, and also instruct. She took care of his women disciples as if they were her own chelas. Besides she had to watch over the proper kind of food and cooking that he and his "sons" needed. One afternoon, for instance, his first disciple, Brahmananda, failed to commune with the Lord as well as usual. That worried the Master considerably. He wanted to know what had gone wrong. After a few moments' cogitation he remarked suddenly, "I know, it is his food!" He rushed to the foot of the tower and called out to the "holy mother," "What did you put in his dinner? My boy's soul is full of sloth. It looks as if he had eaten forbidden food. What did you put in it?" She answered from the window of her tower: "My Lord, thinking that it would do his body good, I put in some extra dabs of butter. I am sorry." At this admission on her part Rama Krishna roared with laughter. However he was glad to know that it was the extra amount of butter, and not rank materialism, that was weighing down the soul of his disciple.

Along with feeding and caring for him and

his disciples, she took lessons in meditation from the Master. And a legend has it that when he started to train her in Advaita yoga —science of Oneness—he found out that she had already advanced very far on the path of Sadhana (Realisation) through her own exertions. It did not take her long to attain Illumination under his guidance. As soon as that had happened, Rama Krishna taught her all he knew. There was nothing that she failed to master. Though she was silent and averse to publicity, yet her fame spread amongst the Hindu women from year to year. Some came to her with their problems; some came to confide to her their secret longing for realization; and many came to her to grant them boons, for they believed that she had the power to do miracles. However the upshot of the matter was that around her grew that nucleus of brave and deeply religious women who started to reform Indian society from within.

When Rama Krishna died, the direction of even his male disciples fell into her hands. All of them say that she was their mother as Rama Krishna was their father. The common people explain the matter beautifully: "Rama Krishna left an eagle's nest full of eaglets. It was his widow, the holy mother, who watched and protected them till they had learned to fly."

Since her life is uniquely interesting, no one can write of it in a few hundred words. Though she died in 1920, yet it was not until last year that the chroniclers succeeded in assembling all the materials for her biography. They all agree that her life-story will be nearly as interesting a spiritual document as that of Rama Krishna.

CHAPTER V

RAMA KRISHNA AND OTHER RELIGIONS

NOW that Rama Krishna had become a Master, like bees to the flower many earnest religious souls came to receive instructions from him. They came from all walks of life. Social reformers, University students, Brahmins, Rajahs, artisans, peasants, Buddhists, Christians and Mohammedans—all flocked to Dakshineswar. Many came out of curiosity. But there were some who came to embrace the new religion of the new Teacher.

After they had held converse with him everyone realised that Rama Krishna had nothing new to say. In fact what he did say sounded simple to the extent of being commonplace. But they, one and all, felt that what he said was nothing compared to what he withheld. "It was his being," says one of those visitors, "that gripped us. His realisation was tiger-strong. As in the jungle when the tiger goes about, even the leaves stop trembling in his presence, so did we feel in the presence of the Master. And after we had left and gone home then we realised what he had done to our souls. For days afterwards we were not the same human beings."

We have already noticed that among the visitors to Dakshineswar there were men who were Christians and Mohammedans. They came to see what "the heathen Rama Krishna" was like. Of course many of them saw in him nothing but a religious man. But there was a Christian who perceived in him a great teacher. He went further than that; he said to Rama Krishna, "You verify to me the teachings of my own religion."

"What is your religion, my son?" asked the Master.

"Christianity, my Lord," answered the gentleman.

Rama Krishna explained, "Yes, *Yata mat*

tato path—As many souls, so many pathways to God. . . . But I have never studied your particular religion. Now I will do so."

From that day on for two years Rama Krishna studied Christianity. Since he did not know English, he had the New Testament read to him in translation, many times over. Gradually it had such an effect on him that he began to meditate on the Christos. He lived like a Christian anchorite, all alone, in the famous woods of Panchabati. Then one day, after many months, he came out and proclaimed, "I found God at the end of the road of Christianity. So if anyone follows Christ he will reach God. I have verified it."

Another time a Mohammedan visitor said to him: "You are the most devout Mohammedan I know!" That roused the Master. He decided to spend some time studying Mohammedanism. Forthwith he had himself converted to that religion. Again he retired into Panchabati to meditate on what had been taught him from the Koran by his Mohammedan teacher. Months passed. Then he came out of his seclusion and proclaimed: "That road too leads to the palace of the same King. Religions differ in their appearance, but not in their essence. No matter which path you take it will usher you in the end into His Presence: the end of all!'

"As the many-colored rivers tear and claw their way to the ocean, and are lost in its steady emerald level, so all the religions, turgid with dogmatism, lose themselves in the serenity of God. Since religions are but means to finding Him, why quarrel about their respective merits and defects? That will take you nowhere."

By now the entire countryside became aware that Rama Krishna had become a universal holy man. An English Christian missionary who had heard all kinds of reports came to investigate him. The legend has it that he came with an interpreter. This sun-ripe, red-faced man from Europe had no sooner sat down in the presence of the Master than he was told, "I salute Lord Jesus Christ as an Incarnation." The abruptness of that statement filled the missionary with embarrassment. He asked, "What do you know about Him?"

Rama Krishna: "Why, I have seen Him in my meditations. His protection spreads like an umbrella over your head. All you Christians are safe from the sun of materialism and the rain of sin under that umbrella."

Missionary: "Are there others under whom people can be safe? Are there other—umbrellas?"

Rama Krishna: "No doubt. There are those who are under prophets that went before Christ. There are other Incarnations of God who are continually looking after their believers. They are just as real as your Lord."

Missionary: "You are wrong. There is only one Son of God."

However, some time later an Indian Christian named Prabhudayal Misra came to see Rama Krishna. Misra was a Christian holy man. His reputation was that of a saint.

No sooner had he seated himself before Rama Krishna than he propounded: "It is the Lord who shines through every creature."

The Master answered very slowly: "The Lord is one, but He is called by a thousand names."

"But I believe Jesus is God Himself."

"Do you see any visions?" questioned Rama Krishna.

The Christian holy man answered: "I used to see effulgence. But later I beheld Jesus. No word can describe His beauty. There is no woman, nor man, nor anything else on earth to equal that beauty, when the Invisible breaks the folds of the visible and reveals Himself."

Rama Krishna sat silent. None spoke. Misra kept still as the rest.

After what seemed hours, Misra felt the force of the Master's Being. He rose to go. He said: "I feel the same power behind you as I perceived in my own Savior's Face. Can you tell me if there is any difference?"

Rama Krishna is reported to have said: "It is the One Flame: eyes of men see it in different colors."

Misra exclaimed: "I would like to surrender everything to you, and follow you."

Rama Krishna forbade him. "No, no. Follow your own unique path. The light that you see now will be dimmed by the greater brightness that It will shed further ahead. Go on; stop not till the End is reached."

It must be borne in mind that the reader cannot identify Rama Krishna with any sect. He did not preach a religion. He lived such a life that it verified the inner reality of all religions. And what is more important is that each man must develop from his own unique heritage a full spiritual life of his own. Though Rama Krishna inherited Hinduism, he developed a unique soul-experience whose magnitude went beyond the limits of any one religion. He lived so that by his example a Mohammedan was heartened to be a better Mohammedan, a Christian a better Christian, and a Buddhist a better Buddhist. This was not the outcome of a wishy-washy eclecticism, but a realization achieved after years of spiritual experiments that he made with all those religions. Not only did he master the inner meaning of the great religions, but also that of the small denominations. For instance, Rama Krishna experimented and experienced the soul-illumination promised by several minor sects of India. One time he spent some months as a Vaishnava—worshipper of Vishnu the Preserver of the world. Another time he got someone to initiate him into the mysteries of Rama pantha. One of the great medieval Rama-panthi (Rama worshipping) saints was Tulsidas whose Ramayana (quite a mystical work) is sung—thousands of lines at a time—by the Hindu mothers to their children, by the minstrels to their audiences, and by many mystics to their disciples.

After experiencing the ecstasies promised by Vaishnavism (Vishnu-worship) and Rama pantha (Rama-worship), Rama Krishna said: "I went by two different roads, but found myself at the end before the same King." Yet he maintained that he who calls God Rama must go on doing so, as must those who call Him Vishnu, Jehova, Christ, or Nirvana.

Then one of his disciples asked him: "If all those names mean the One Person, why not use one name only? Why should sects insist on their little names?" In answer, the Master told a story. "When Rama, the Incarnation of God, was in difficulty, his servant and devotee Hanuman, the monkey, sought to extricate his Lord. But he could not do so unaided by Garuda, the thunder-bird, friend and servant of Vishnu. After having rendered his aid, Garuda prayed Rama to appear in the form he (Garuda) knew. Lo! suddenly Rama became Vishnu. After his adoration of Vishnu, Garuda flapped his lightning wings and flew away into the silence of the sky. Then suddenly Vishnu changed into Rama and asked Hanuman the monkey if he could worship the Lord appearing in the Vishnu form.

"Hanuman said with tears in his eyes and love in his voice: '*Shrinathe Janaki Nathe*— I know that the two forms are of the One Beloved, yet to me the form of Rama is everything. It is Rama's feet that is my home, it is Rama that is the chalice of my salvation. Oh! my Beloved, avert not from mine eyes Thy Face of Rama!"

Thus did Rama Krishna answer his disciple: "Unto each soul its own Image of God."

According to a legend, to those who cared for his opinion of the seven great religions of the world, Rama Krishna said: "The scriptures are right. God incarnates amongst men irrespective of time and place. Whenever righteousness is stoned to death and the unrighteous rule the earth, He is born amongst men, as a man, to bring about the victory of Truth, Love, and Wisdom. Buddha, Jesus, Mohammed, and Krishna were such incarnations."

"Are we likely to have incarnations of God in the future?"

Rama Krishna: "Yes. Who are you to shut the door of the future in the face of the oncoming God? The future is surprise-wombed. If rascals and demons can be foaled of that womb, why not God? He will come again and again irrespective of sex and age whenever men need Him!"

The same legend gives an instance of Rama Krishna's way of interpreting some passages of the New Testament. There were some of his visitors who took exception to those beatitudes which extolled the mourners and the poor in spirit.

They said: "We do not know what they mean mystically. But from the intellectual point of view the mourners are a wretched lot. So are the poor in spirit." The Master answered: "But if you look at it from the point of view of Realisation it is the truth. Suppose you mourn for God day in and day out. Imagine a mother-cat whose kitten has been taken out of her basket and put elsewhere by a mischievous boy. Does she not wail and mourn till her voice reaches her lost one who in turn answers her. And in a short time they find each other. So is the Mourner of God. He has lost his Infinite Child. He must wail and cry till the Child of Silence cries and reveals Himself to the seeker. Untold human beings have found God that way.

"Similarly the poor in spirit. They say to Him 'You are Infinite. You have made me nothing. I will accept no riches, nor glory, save the boundless wealth of beholding You.' If they sincerely go on thinking and praying they will find Him in a short time. And suddenly their nothingness will become the all-inclusive Nothingness of God. God is like the hollow in a cup. It is the hollow that can be filled with water. Call Him Nothing: behold He contains everything. Then if you define Him Everything, He suddenly slips out of your definition, like a song-bird from a broken cage, proclaiming His eternal homelessness in things.

"Oh, no; you must not stop with an intellectual criticism of what any incarnation of God said about the poor in spirit. You must meditate on it till you tear to pieces what he said and find under it—with the eye of Realisation—what he meant. The incarnations of God never speak one langauge: they always use two—that of sound and silence: Vision and Realisation."

It is a pity that the commentaries that Rama Krishna made on the New Testament, the Koran, and other holy books have not been preserved.

CHAPTER VI

ORTHODOX HINDUS AND RAMA KRISHNA

WHEN he was about thirty-six Rama Krishna settled down to elucidate his religious experiences to those who wished to hear him. Now that he had had his supreme Realisation he hoped to train some earnest souls besides his own wife.

But earnest souls are rare in this world. And those who came to him at first were either social reformers, or orthodox Brahmins and hide-bound ritualists who wanted him to help them in their pet practices. Not that they were luke-warm believers, but because they emphasized the letter more than the spirit of religious rites. Rama Krishna castigated them mercilessly. He pursued the same course with those social reformers who sought to drown the soul's hunger for God in a turbid philosophy of Humanitarianism. If the bigoted begged Rama Krishna to lead a crusade for orthodoxy, the emancipated sought to enslave him to their cause of freedom. Small wonder then that he who had the whole truth had no encouragement for the votaries of half-truths. He said again and again: "Religion is a road to lead you to God. A road is not a house; you don't live on the edge of it like shop-keepers vending your wares, each praising his own and denouncing his neighbor's products. Get to the end of the road and behold the Endless. For He alone can extinguish the fire of your quarrels."

One might think that his severe judgments would keep people from coming to him. On the contrary, they flocked to see Rama Krishna in ever-increasing numbers.

First of all let us see what Rama Krishna had to say to those pious Hindus whose religious sincerity was above reproach, and whose orthodoxy had not yet dimmed the light of their soul. Such an one, according to a legend, was Ishan Mukherjee, a very rich, good Brahmin. Ishan was a whole-hearted believer in Karma yoga—realising one's salvation through deeds. All his life he had served his fellow men. If there was a hospital to build, or an orphan asylum to maintain, the community found in Ishan a ready and whole-hearted supporter of such schemes. His benevolence was untiring. He was an orthodox Brahmin in the true sense of the word: he lived not for himself but for those who needed him. His fellow men considered him one of the Lord's elect.

But the man himself was not quite sure of that. So in order to find out how one really earns salvation, one afternoon he sought counsel of the Holy One of Dakshineswar. He found Rama Krishna seated on the Ghaut discoursing to a small group of men, while beyond on the Ganges boats drew their bulging sails of turquoise and ochre against the scorching gold of the sunset sky.

Ishan bowed to the Master and took the dust from his feet. After that a hush fell on the gathering.

Since Rama Krishna alone had the privilege he at last broke the silence: "What brings you here, O Brahmin?"

Ishan said: "Search of salvation, my Lord. I do all that the shastras (scriptures) prescribe. I observe all the rituals. But the knowledge that I seek is not in books. It abides in the tiger-mouth of a realised soul."

But Rama Krishna, the same legend continues, did not answer at once. Seeing that the hour of Arati was fast approaching, he got up and went to the Kali temple. The others too left. But Ishan remained. He began saying his prayers. The sun set. The boats, the river, the farther shore, slowly sank into the inky stillness of the night. Suddenly like a flock of birds the stars preened their silver wings in the dark sky.

It was about an hour later when the moon had begun to rise that Rama Krishna returned from the Kali temple. He said to Ishan who was waiting for him: "Rituals and routines of worship, if they do not make the heart sing with joy, are of no earthly use. The flower falls from the tree as the fruit appears. So must fall away rituals and prayers like shackles from a liberated soul. Salvation to the soul is what freedom is to a prisoner."

"But is there no salvation in Karma—doing of good deeds?" questioned Ishan the Brahmin.

Rama Krishna answered: "There is salvation through every path whether of deeds, knowledge, or love."

Ishan quoted, "The scriptures say 'He who with steadfast love loves Me (God) will know Me. He who with obdurate knowledge pursues Me, the seed eternal blossoming in all beings, will find Me the end of all knowledge. And he who acts so that he desires no earthly fruits of his actions, will find Me the fulfiller of all deeds.' "

Rama Krishna is reported to have answered: "Yes, Ishan, the scriptures are right. But how many men can act for the sake of doing the perfect deed without any hope of earthly results? Also scholarship—like a lamp—if it does not contain the flame of longing for the Infinite knowledge of the Infinite God, cannot give freedom to a soul. The same is the case with the love of God; like a bird if it is not voiced with an excruciating longing for Him, it will not sing the perfect melody of salvation. Knowledge, deeds and love—each one of them has to be selfless in order to find the Self of God."

Ishan commented to himself, though not in silence, "No matter what path a soul takes, it is strewn with the thorns and pebbles of selflessness."

"No matter what means a Soul adopts—deeds, knowledge, or love—it must be kept under the tiger-claw subjection to the end: the Endless," emphasized Rama Krishna.

Ishan wailed, "Then what am I to do?"

Rama Krishna began quietly: "Have you noticed the steady flame of a lamp? The slightest stir in the air will make it flicker. Just as delicate is the task of seeking God. No matter how selfless your deeds—outwardly they may appear perfect—but if within you stirs the slightest feeling of self or desire, it will destroy your realisation of God as the wind blows out the candle."

"But how is one to be free of desire to that high degree?"

Rama Krishna answered: "Stop listening to the flattery of the priests. Do not for a moment think that your deeds are going to do anybody any good. Begin at the beginning. Purify your deeds of any taint of self by purifying your thoughts. More than that—purify your dreams too. Desire steals into men even when they are asleep. I have experienced it myself. In the early days of my spiritual activity though I purified my conscious moments of all taints of self, yet I could not free my sleep from its clutches. Desire used to steal into me through my dreams. It took years; but at last I succeeded in achieving total purity. You will not advance your soul towards God to the extent even of a child's footprint if you do not become selfless in dreams as well as in your thoughts. The way most people act, to know and love God is a scandal. They think He is hungrier than a common beggar at their door, easy to satisfy with a handful of any kind of offering. Oh, no; He cannot be fooled by little sacrifices when desire for earthly results stalk through men's thoughts and dreams like herds of elephants through a jungle. And do you think you can satisfy God by presenting Him with a fraction of your self? He, being Infinite, will not accept anything but the infinite in you."

"So," interrupted Ishan, "it is not enough that we are pure in our waking moments. We have to be free of desire while lying unconscious in our sleep. How can one attain such unalloyed purity?"

Rama Krishna answered: "Pray and meditate. Only undertake those actions that fall within the limits of your purified thoughts and dreams. Eschew any action that is tainted in the slightest by self. Give up building hospitals, houses for the helpless and other charitable institutions. Seek not to flatter yourself with gigantic deeds. Undertake duties as small in size as your self-surrender to God. Then as your selflessness and purity grow—and things of the Soul grow very fast—it will pierce its own way through the material world and benefit others as the

Ganges sprang through the hard rocks of the Himalayas and watered thousands of miles with her beneficence."

"Is there anything else I can do? Need I study books? Need I practise love of God?" asked Ishan all in one breath. The Master was amused by his breathless hurry.

"Because you want God why should you give up harmless amusements? Read all you want, love all you can. But see that you grow more selfless through it all. And when you become One with Him you will find that He exceeds all books. He is infinite knowledge, and all Love. If your God realised through deeds excludes knowledge and love, then he is a false God. The true God includes all. There is only one thing that He excludes, and that is desire for results whether here on earth or in Heaven. Renounce all earthly results, give up even the hope of the felicity of Heaven, Swarga."

"Why, my Lord?" questioned Ishan with trepidation.

Rama Krishna: "You are a reader of

books. You ought to know what the scriptures say on such matters."

Ishan pondered a while then said that there was a stanza in the Gita that condemned good actions if done for results here or hereafter: "'*Yami Mam puspitam bacham* . . . The purport of it is that:

'Men who are full of desires and look upon Heaven as their highest goal are not going to attain salvation.'

I have read that, my Lord. But I do not know what it truly means. Does it really mean something?"

Rama Krishna: "If you give up the desire for hospitals here, why should you wish to have a palace in Paradise? If the leprosy of desire ruins all here, far worse will be its havoc in Heaven!"

"I do not understand, my Lord," exclaimed Ishan.

Rama Krishna explained: "If you defeat your soul's end by doing good deeds with earthly results in view, you will do it endless harm if you act in order to be rewarded hereafter. Selflessness is not only the road out of earthliness but also out of Heaven. Does God abide in one and only one place? No. He cannot be chained either to Heaven or to earth. And if you fasten your soul's claws on Him, you will have to give up the selfish joys of Paradise too."

"Then what happens to the acts of beneficence we do on earth? Are they at all permanent? What happens to them if they do not bring us nearer Heaven? Can we do any good to anybody?" asked Ishan in amazement.

"Those who do lasting benefits to their neighbours are men selfless as God. God is infinite and endless, hence His creation has no end. Persons who have renounced their little selves and have attained the Self of God are the ones whose creations can not perish.

"No man can achieve deathless deeds if he is attached in the slightest to anything less than the Purusha (Infinite). When your Self is all burnt up and God has taken possession of you completely then every act of your life will be immortal. Whether you seek Jnana yoga, realisation through knowledge, or Karma yoga, realisation through deeds, you have to have a dire longing for God at its foundation. Without that foundation the house of knowledge is a perpetual labyrinth of deception, and the temple of deeds is but the tabernacle of self-adulation. Therefore go to-night: lift yourself like an offering to the Self of the Universe. With that act of surrender you will begin to build the palace of immortal acts. With those hands of yours doomed to death you shall erect the citadel of deathlessness."

Ishan was deeply moved by the Master's last words. He slowly bowed and took the dust from the latter's feet. In deep silence he walked into the moonlit night.

CHAPTER VII

RAMA KRISHNA AND A MODERN SOCIAL REFORMER

I THINK the reader has heard of Brahmoism, the name Unitarianism bears in India. If translated literally it means One-Godism. And people who profess it call their society Brahmo-Samaj, or, the Society of One God. It was a movement that began a little before Rama Krishna was born, and had its full tide during his lifetime. One of the greatest Brahmos, Keshup Chunder Sen, was a devoted friend of the saint of Dakshineswar. It is his conversations with Keshub Sen and his attitude toward Brahmoism that will give the reader another view of Rama Krishna's religious outlook.

But let us begin with a history of Brahmoism and its founder, Ram Mohun Roy. During the early years of the British rule in India, there rose a very great man amongst the Hindus. His name was Ram Mohun Roy. He was six feet tall, and strong as a tiger. His mind was correspondingly vigorous. In fact until Dyananda, a Punjabi holy man, and Rama Krishna, who appeared about fifty years after him, India had no man like Ram Mohun Roy. In the early twenties of the last century he, a youth of twenty-four, saw a Suttee, a widowed relative of his burnt to death with her husband's corpse. A Brahmin of fiery temperament and a scholar of great repute, he started then and there the movement to abolish Suttee. Since I have explained the origin of Suttee in my book, *Caste and Outcast,* I shall not go into it here. But it was Ram Mohun Roy who began the first tremendous attack against it. He proved from the Scriptures of Hinduism that no such custom is sanctioned by them. Since he was a keen Sanscrit scholar he went from temple to temple and from one Sanscrit Tol, college, to another, rousing the teachers' and priests' horror by expounding to them the utterly irreligious nature of Suttee. They all agreed that "Suttee is a social custom several hundred years old; it has had nothing to do with our Scriptures and creed."

Just at the height of his fight against Suttee, Ram Mohun had this good fortune; the then British Governor General of India also wanted to abolish it. Since the British sovereign power alone had the authority to pass a law, all the Indian reformers, headed by Ram Mohun and his associates, sought its help. Before Ram Mohun was a man of forty, Suttee had been abolished from India.

Having discovered that a firmly established social and supposedly religious custom like Suttee had no foundation in the Hindu scriptures, he was determined to explore further into the origins of Hindu society and religion. He not only studied in India but went as far as Thibet in search of exact and accurate Sanskrit texts. In those days, Thibet was symbolic of No Man's Land. After a sojourn of half a dozen years there, he returned to India. He found Western missionaries attacking Hindu religion as a heathen affair of no consequence. In order to know the basis of their criticism, Ram

Mohun learnt Latin and Greek. He now read the Bible in those languages. Incidentally he studied Arabic in order to read the Koran in the original. And he brought to bear on those alien scriptures—Mohammedan and Christian—the light of the Upanishads and the Vedas, with the result that in all the religions that one sentence of the Upanishads burnt like a steady flame:

EKAM SAT
VIPRA BAHUDHA VADANTI

"THERE IS ONLY ONE GOD, IT IS MEN WHO HAVE GIVEN HIM MANY NAMES."

He came to the conclusion that all religions preach the same inner experience:—

Jesus says—"THE KINGDOM OF GOD IS WITHIN YOU."

Mohammed—"HE DWELLS WITHIN YOUR VERY SOULS AND YE SEE HIM NOT."

The Upanishad—"HE IS THE DWELLER WITHIN YOU" and "HOMINUM INTERIORE HABITAT VERITAS" says the Latin Neo-Platonist.

After he noticed the resemblances of all the religions, Ram Mohun set down their differences as so much nonsense, and at once started to preach Brahmoism—the religion of One God Who is above the battling claims of religions and priests. This Indian brand of Unitarianism owes nothing to external sources. Its indebtedness, all of it, lies at the door of Ram Mohun Roy. Soon after launching his movement in India, the founder of Indian Unitarianism went to Europe to discern in its dark night of Christian fanaticism some dawning light of tolerance and brotherhood. Unfortunately soon after his arrival in Europe, Ram Mohun died. Thus ended the life of India's first missionary to the West.

At his death Brahmoism passed under the leadership of Keshub Chunder Sen. I have already intimated that Keshub was very fond of Rama Krishna. Now the difference between Keshub and his predecessor, Ram Mohun Roy, lay in two things. First of all, Keshub, unlike the latter, knew little Sanskrit and less Arabic. But he was a master of English. In fact his eloquence in English equaled that of Gladstone. He imbibed many of the bourgeois Victorian English ideas. He had none of Ram Mohun's gaunt and eagle-eyed scholarship and his oriental bringing up. The latter studied the Western thought after he had been nurtured and formed by the old austere Brahmanic training. And when in his mature age he came into contact with Western Philosophy and religion he was all the better equipped to resist whatever weaknesses they had. He praised only their authentic beauty and strength.

But by the time Keshub was in his early teens, English Universities and their English curricula had been started in India. So he was formed and strengthened by Western learning. In other words, Keshub did not drink much of his mother's milk—he was nursed at the breast of a step-mother. So from the start Keshub was a bellicose Occidental ameliorist and a pietistic Hindu. His Unitarianism was not a religion of a scholar's insight. On the contrary to him Unitarianism was a banner of revolt. It was for him to carry that banner high. Hence he became a fiery lecturer, and a passionate social reformer. His religious experiences remained primarily emotional. He wanted to sweep away idolatry and renew the original worship of the One God of the Upanishads. Next, he wished to abolish caste, seclusion of women, and early marriage.

Judging by his portraits Keshub Sen must have been a tall man, light as an Italian in complexion. He had a large oval face, dark brown eyes, and an extremely sensitive but rather weak mouth. He often dressed in English style, and his most impassioned lecture—in it he reached his high-water mark of eloquence—was on Jesus the Man. Those who heard Keshub on Jesus say that in that one lecture he did more for Christianity in India than all the missionaries put together.

Now, let the reader try to imagine the effect that Rama Krishna had on Keshub. It must have been one of unmixed dislike. For Rama Krishna was no iconoclast, nor a reformer of society. I wonder if Keshub came in the company of that other Unitarian, Mazoondar, the author of the Oriental Christ. It was

Mazoondar, I think, who was the first Unitarian to say about the holy man of Dakshineswar: "Before I met Rama Krishna I had a poor conception of religion—I spent my time rampaging about reforms. But now that I have known him I know what a true life of religion consists of."

Attracted by such words of praise from a fellow-Brahmo of importance, Keshub at last paid Rama Krishna a visit. He had come prepared to find a superstitious backward Hindu. Then lo and behold! "Here was a man who was the true son of Immortality." A man who had not much intellectual training, no contact with any European books or persons, yet how well he could converse on important spiritual matters. Whence did he derive his knowledge? Keshub was shocked and surprised. He could not believe that while Ram Mohun Roy had been wrestling with the Scriptures of all the religions and eliciting their real meaning from them, here was this Rama Krishna battling with the Divine Mother to wrest from Her lips the Secret of Life and Death. That cult of tolerance that Ram Mohun Roy found through hard processes of reasoning and study, Rama Krishna had lived these many years! What a surprise indeed! Was it the two halves of One Reality that he was seeing? Was Ram Mohun the scholar of unity and brotherhood, and Rama Krishna the exemplary life of it? Such was the effect produced by Rama Krishna on Keshub.

It was not very long before the two men became fast friends. Here I shall give some of Rama Krishna's characteristic talks with Keshub, for that alone can illustrate how the holy man respected and emphasized the uniqueness of his friend's character. He aimed to strengthen Keshub in his own light and not to change him.

On their first meeting Rama Krishna said to Keshub: "I hear that you have had a vision of God. I wish to learn of it from your lips." Thus began a long discussion which ended with this story from the Holy One. "Everyone conceives God in the light of his own experience. Some men saw a chameleon going up a tree. One of them followed it to the top, then climbed down. He proclaimed to his friends 'That lizard is green.' Then another man went up the tree to see the animal with his own eyes. He came down and reported 'That animal is red.' The third man did likewise and reported the lizard to be blue. Thus started an altercation that threatened to be bloody. A passer-by came along; noticing those persons raising such a tumult, he inquired as to what was the matter. They told him their trouble. He said, 'Oh, that chameleon! He lives on that tree under which I sleep. He does not wear the same color long—sometimes he is blue, sometimes green, and sometimes utterly colorless.' So is God," concluded Rama Krishna. "He is of infinite appearances."

After that story, suddenly, like a bolt from the blue, he said: "Keshub, your tail has dropped off." Then he explained, "You must have noticed how tadpoles are doomed to swim in the water until their tails drop off; and in a trice they become frogs. As the tail is to a tadpole, so is ignorance to man. Only he who has dropped his ignorance hops upon the shore of God-consciousness. I feel that you are such a man. Though you live in the world yet you can enjoy divine bliss."

After their first meeting Keshub came to see the Master frequently. But in spite of their growing intimacy during the early stages of their friendship Rama Krishna had the feeling that the Brahmo leader was not inclined to put much trust in "the superstitious holy man." Rama Krishna whenever Keshub asked his opinion on religious matters generally prefaced his remarks thus: "Keshub, of course I will say what comes to my mind. But you can cut off its head and tail and accept what is agreeable to you."

Though in course of time the Holy One came to love Keshub dearly, yet he could not stomach the characteristics of many of his followers. What was most jarring to Rama Krishna was their copying the Protestant service. Rama Krishna makes fun of it thus: "I went to Keshub's religious service. After a sermon on the glory of God, the Leader said: 'Let us commune with Him.' I thought, 'They will now go into the inner world and stay a long time.' Hardly had a few minutes passed when they all opened their eyes. I was astonished. Can anyone find Him after so slight a meditation? After it was all over, when we were alone, I spoke to Keshub about it: 'I watched all of your congregation communing with their eyes shut. You know what it reminded me of? Sometimes in Dakshineswar I have seen under the trees a flock of monkeys sitting stiff and looking the very picture of innocence. But their thoughts belied the picture they made: they were thinking and planning their campaign of robbing certain gardens of fruits, roots and other edibles. Oh! yes, they were thinking of swooping down on those unprotected gardens in a few moments. The communing that your followers did with God to-day is no more serious than were those monkeys trying to look innocent of mischief!"

There is a song of the Brahmos in which occurs the line: "Think and worship Him every moment of the day." Rama Krishna hearing it, stopped the singer and commented: "Change that line into 'Pray and worship

Him only twice a day.' Say what you really will do. Why fib to the Infinite?"

There was one particular habit of Keshub's that he criticised the most, namely, ornate praise of the many glories of the Lord. So one day, unable to bear the catalogue of God's glories enumerated by Keshub, Rama Krishna blurted out: "Why do you give such statistics about His powers and the attributes that He possesses? Does a son say to his father's face, 'Oh, my father, you own so many houses, so many horses, so many cows, gardens and grottos?' Does that take in any father? It is natural that a father should feed, protect, and put all his resources at the disposal of his sons. We are His sons. That He should be kind, beneficent, merciful, forgiving, etc., is natural, and not a matter of surprise. If you think of Him and His estate as such a matter of surprise, you can never be intimate with Him; you cannot draw close and demand of Him the vision of His Face. Don't think of Him so that He must necessarily be remote from us. Conceive Him as your nearest, then He will reveal Himself to you! Don't you think his attributes that you dilate on make you idolatrous?"

"I do not see the connection between the two," protested the great reformer. "Idolatry is worship of stones, images, icons and other inanimate forms. God cannot abide in them. He is formless."

"But Keshub," pleaded Rama Krishna, "God is both. He is in form and formlessness. Images and other symbols of Him are as valid and vivid as your strings of divine attributes. Attributes of Him are chill hard forms. They are not different from what you call idolatry."

According to the legend-makers Keshub retorted in a spirited fashion: "I cannot agree with you. When it comes to flat idolatry and other sordid accretions that have come to be called Hinduism, I consider you to be in the wrong." Keshub always spoke in long periods. "Child-widows, caste-system, Purdah (seclusion of women), worship of sticks and stones, and soulless priestcraft are abominations that must be swept out of existence. Must man, who is God on earth, bend the knee to trees and totems? Is that religion? Do you dare call it spiritual? No, dear Master, the storm that I am raising must cleanse the foul sky of Hinduism so that our children can be called human beings and not dumb beasts who are driven from pillar to post by the cunning of priests and the greed of innumerable Gods."

"But Keshub," commented the Master, "the foul sky, as you call Hinduism, cannot be cleansed by a storm of invectives. That may change the appearance of things, but it is beyond its power to improve reality. Real improvements are wrought by blessings. Can you let loose upon us a flood of blessings that will touch and transfigure every shore of our life?"

"What do you exactly mean?" asked Keshub.

"You are a scholar; you can instruct us as to what Incarnations of God did when they were on earth. Please tell us," requested Rama Krishna.

Keshub acceded readily. "If you take Lord Buddha, in Him you find an apt illustration of your point. He never lost His temper; nor did He criticise His opponents. On the contrary, He blessed one and all that came to Him. In fact His vast sympathy, boundless love, and austere morality, no matter whom they touched, made him a better and finer human being. Is that what you call the blessings of a God-man which change the world? Is that what Being means?"

"What other name can we give that power in an Incarnation of God?"

"Ah, dear Master," ejaculated Keshub, "your snare has caught me, I feel that you are right. Only God in us can bring out the God that is in others."

"Keshub, your speech ravishes me!" exclaimed the Master. A glint of exaltation danced in Rama Krishna's eyes. He ceased speaking.

Silence like a palpable something fell upon the audience. It lasted a long time. The air grew pregnant with a strange presence. Rama Krishna's face slowly altered. It threw away its usual mask-like expression. Instead, as a smoking brazier begins to burn, an intense glow spread over his whole countenance.

Slowly his lips parted. No matter how commonplace his thoughts, they sounded invincible now. An indescribable sweetness hung over every word he uttered.

"Men think that to criticise is to give life. A eunuch's denunciation of barrenness does not produce a child. To create is to be like God. One must be all essence! When you are filled with the essence of all existence then whatever you say becomes true. Poets have praised virtue and truth; has that made their readers virtuous and truthful?

"On the contrary, when a selfless person lives amongst us his deeds become the very heart-beat of virtue. The being of such a one hovers over the world on wings of benediction. He becomes the chalice of holiness. Whatever he does to others improves even their meanest dreams. Men in their amazement pay their homage by calling him an incarnation of God. Like God, whatever he touches becomes true and pure. He becomes the father of reality. What he creates never flounders in time. That is what I expect you to do, Keshub. Silence the dogs of invectives!

Let the elephant of Being trumpet its blessings on all! You have that power; will you use it? Or, shall you squander this life-time by abusing people? Shall men say that Keshub spent his days in the tavern of talk, drinking the wine of eloquence? On the contrary may you BE so that they will say 'He dwelt amongst us like a tiger of truth. Wherever he went errors trembled like leaves in the jungle, and sin fled before him like a herd of goats. He was so full of blessings that even his feeblest gestures showered love on all. His words were immortalities. He did not humble us with criticisms; for he heightened us with God.' "

All these criticisms instead of hurting Keshub made him love Rama Krishna. That shows how noble that leader of the Brahmo-Samaj really was. Month after month they met and discussed everything between them—Christ, Buddha, Zöroaster, Mohammed, and other Incarnations of God who had blessed all mankind.

At last Keshub fell ill. Rama Krishna went to see him very often, and talked about the

Lord for hours at a time. One day, perceiving that Keshub would not live long, Rama Krishna intimated to him the approaching end. With tears in his eyes he said:

"Keshub, the Master Gardener treats the Basra (rose) plant severely because it produces the best of flowers. The Master trims it, sometimes takes it out, root and all; then exposes it to the sun and frost. You are going to be replanted. For the Gardener wants magnificent blossoms from you!" Then Rama Krishna left his bedside. In a while, when the news of Keshub's death reached him, the Holy One said: "I have lost one so intimate to myself that I feel as if half of me had perished."

It is fitting that this chapter should close with a statement of Rama Krishna's belief in Immortality.

One day a friend of his, Mani Mallik, lost his son. So he came to Rama Krishna for some consolation soon after the obsequies were over. The reception room was full of people to whom Rama Krishna was talking. But no sooner had Mallik appeared in his mourning dress than the utterly unrelieved whiteness of it fell on that assembly like the crash of a bolt. However, after Mallik had seated himself, Rama Krishna began to talk, which helped to put all his listeners at their ease. Then he stopped. A peaceful hush followed. As the humming of insects disturbs the morning air the assembly heard a soft murmur fretting the silence that had fallen a short while ago. It was Mallik who was telling Rama Krishna his sorrow in a very low tone of voice. The Holy One, perceiving that the crowd was trying to catch Mallik's words, rose to his feet and began to sing and dance.

> Oh Soul, lift the lance of Truth,
> Don your coat of mail!
> For behold! death the enemy
> Has pierced your citadel.

Thus he went on, singing, dancing, and speaking. There was no doubt now that he was acting a mystery play, in which the human soul goes to war, and conquers death. When that was over he sat down by Mallik and said: "It is a terrible pain you are feeling.

But it is not the sorrow inflicted by the sword of Truth, but of a body for another like itself. But these physical forms suffer as long as they live—and no more. The soul, that scimitar of Truth, never suffers.

"Once I saw a man die. It was my own dear nephew, Akshoy. I watched him carefully. Suddenly the sword was removed from its scabbard which lay there dead. But that made no difference to the sharp blade. What I saw gave me joy. I laughed and danced. After the body was cremated the next day, standing on that verandah yonder I felt as if someone was wringing my heart as a man wrings a water-soaked towel. Then I said, 'But, Divine Mother, if I who have renounced the world feel so much pain, how much more suffer those who live in it!' Ah! thus I tasted a fraction of what you are feeling now, my friend. But you, if you cling to God, you will not go under in your deepest sorrow. Behold the small vessels on the Ganges, they are upset by a small wave, but a barge glides over the largest waves with ease. Oh! great barge of the Soul, load yourself deeply with God, then you will not be shaken by sorrows even mountain-high. It is the scabbard, the body, wailing for the body, not the sword, the Soul, tempered with the Immortality of God." It was not those words only, but the man who spoke them, who moved Mallik so that he rose to go saying: "I knew I had to come to you, for no one else could have quenched my pain."

"Those who are attached to earthliness fear death. But he who is not cross-eyed through earthliness sees no death. Many times with mine eyes straightened by meditation I stood on the border contemplating the two mansions: life here and life beyond. There was no death separating the two. So lose your earthliness and your attachment to things; then suddenly you will find Life as one. There is no such interruption as death."

CHAPTER VIII

RAMA KRISHNA AND HIS DISCIPLES

THOUGH Rama Krishna's contacts with the multitude were very interesting, yet until one studies the choice and training of his disciples, one cannot grasp the unique significance of his message.

Unlike the prophets of the past he had no taste for evangelism. Time and again he is reported to have said:

"Those days are gone when a teacher's inspired speech made people see God. We have to build on other foundations now. We must live such an intense inner life that it will become a Being. And Being will send forth untold torches of Truth. Rivers rise and rush because their sire, the mountain, sits still. It took God ages and ages to make mountains, but generations and leagues have been bathed, fed and sustained by their streams ever since.

"Let us make a Being—raise a mountain of God in our midst no matter how long it takes, and when it will have been reared it will pour rivers of compassion and light on all men for all time."

With that philosophy in mind let us now examine the way Rama Krishna trained some of his disciples. Courtesy forbids our exploration of the lives of his disciples still living. We shall confine ourselves to the study of the life-events of those who are dead. Regarding two of them, Brahmananda and Turyananda, our knowledge is fragmentary; for they died recently, and the materials of their life-story have not yet been gathered together. That compels us to concentrate on the lives of Vivekananda, Premananda, and Lattu Maharaj. About these three not a great deal is known since they—being monks who had renounced this world—have left us only as much of their own temporal history as they could not destroy. Anyone who has read Vivekananda's life of Rama Krishna is perfectly aware that he says nothing of the intimate and eventful moments between himself and his Master. The same thing holds true of the other disciples of Rama Krishna: in none of their memoirs does one find any record of the writer's own spiritual experiences. That is what makes the writing of their lives a difficult, if not an arid task.

However, we must gather all the meager details that have been left us by those holy men. First of all the reader must bear in mind that Rama Krishna, who was hospitable and generous to the whole world, was extremely strict in the choice of his disciples.

They were chosen mostly from young University men who came from diverse castes. Almost all of them knew at least one foreign language and had a thorough knowledge of Sanskrit. Once when he was asked why he accepted young men of such excellent parts, the Master said: "They are not yet caught in the net of desire, nor caged in wealth. They are wholly unattached. Their character is good. . . . Then why do you assume that I choose my chelas? The Divine Mother brings them to me. It is She who draws them. I but train those whom She chooses. It is She who makes me examine their secret habits, their tastes, and distastes. At night while they are asleep I commune; the veils fall from around them, and She the Omniscient, points out to me not only what they are but also the degree of spiritual progress each one of them makes daily. When you see with your soul's insight you see Selves of men and women as you see through the glass the things resting in a glass case beyond your touch and taste. Thus do I make sure of my disciples' characters long before I initiate them."

The following incident proves that Rama Krishna was aware of everything about the spiritual life of his apostles. Saradananda and others testify that one night while the Master was asleep, Vivekananda, Kali Tapasyi, Saradananda, and two others went to the woods to meditate. Before starting to do so Vivekananda said to Kali Tapasyi, "Keep your hand on my shoulder while I meditate in the new way that the Master has taught me."

In about half an hour Kali Tapasyi's hand

began to shake as a rope is shaken by a strong wind. When it was all over they all said to Vivekananda "Anyone who touched you felt a shock like that of an electric battery."

No sooner had they reached the Master's apartment on their return home than out of the darkness they heard him calling. They lit a lamp and went to see him. He said to Vivekananda, "Hardly had you gathered spiritual treasure than you squandered it. Spirituality grows in the soul as a child in the womb. You cannot experiment on its coming to earth until time is ripe. When will you learn that whenever you act foolishly I know all about it? Always ask me before starting your childish and rash experiments."

But to return to Rama Krishna's choice and training of his disciples. Not only did he examine them thoroughly before accepting them, but he also kept a watch on every phase of their life. He accepted for training both householders and unattached persons, yet he insisted on a final public declaration on everyone's part as to the exact nature of his obligations to other human beings.

"For," he said, "let no one suffer want and destitution because you, my son, wish to become a holy man." And he never gave initiation to anyone whose dependents—father, mother, wife, or children—withheld the necessary permissions. Even now the same procedure is followed in the Monastery. They never accept anyone for the monastic life who is not voluntarily given up by his family. For they say that a man who is fleeing from the responsibilities of this world is too weak to be exposed to the more dangerous responsibility of finding God.

The case of Rama Krishna's first disciple, Swami Brahmananda, illustrates all that most amply. When he met the Master he was a rich Brahmin boy of two and twenty. Even at that early age he proved so brilliant and gifted that every important career of life was open to him. Just at that juncture one day some of his curious college friends urged him to accompany them to Dakshineswar to see the holy man. "He came to see what I was like," Rama Krishna said years later. "He must have heard strange stories about here," meaning himself. "But fortunately instead of finding in me a God-chattering monkey, he saw my Self. He came again, alone. In a few days he gave up everything and stayed here like a ram tethered to his post. His people followed. They wanted to know what sort of company he was keeping. They were satisfied after a look at me. But they did not wish the boy to be a monk, for they wanted him to marry and settle down. I was questioned about it. That worried me a bit. But I was sure of the lad's soul; so I wished to see the young lady they had chosen for him. One day the little mother was brought to me. One look at her convinced me that she would help and not hinder his soul's reach for God. I told the blessed little mother who and what she was marrying. She seemed to know all that. As a sound is lost in the silence of Heaven, my worries vanished at once. In a short time Brahmananda married. Now look what a holy man he is! His wife never claimed him. She realised God by giving him freedom to attain Holiness."

After Brahmananda about five more young

men—four of whom are yet living—became Rama Krishna's disciples. Vivekananda was the fifth. In order to know what the ocean tastes like we need but put one drop of it on our tongue, so in order to learn the way Rama Krishna brought up his disciples let us study the case of Vivekananda. For he was typical of all of them; besides, he is not unknown in Europe and America.

From childhood, Vivekananda was brilliant, brave, and versatile. He was one of the Kshatrya (Warrior) caste, and had had a religious bringing up. His forbears lived a very strict orthodox life. His father and grandfather carried religious practices as far as the scriptures enjoined. There was no radicalism in his blood. Heresy in religious matters was unknown to it. But, alas! in his middle teens, Vivekananda developed a strong tendency towards Agnosticism. He believed with the ancient Sanskrit philosopher, Charbaka, that "God does not exist: He is an invention of the priests." Then from Charbakism he went forward and accepted the Vaisheshikha doctrine (Atomism) of Kanada.

Later Kapila's Shankhya all the more confirmed in him his notion that though one must lead a strictly moral life, yet one need not believe in God.

Vivekananda, whose ancestors were fighters, had no sooner convinced himself of Agnosticism than he went to war for it. But in order to fight successfully one must have followers and friends. The orthodox Hindu society furnished him with none. Then instead of despairing, he went ahead and joined the Brahmos under Keshub Sen whose zeal for social reform Vivekananda shared. Thus before he was twenty years old he became known as an iconoclast who was a fanatical puritan. And all of his contemporaries affirm that he had no respect for anything save the true and the moral. Vivekananda took special delight in going out of his way to attack the pretensions of learned holy men and Brahmins. He was a sort of agnostic bull in the china shop of religion.

One day in the company of Keshub Sen, Vivekananda came to Dakshineswar. One of the eye-witnesses of that visit (the late Bhupendranath Basu) describes the meeting of Rama Krishna and Vivekananda:

"Vivekananda and I were studying the Law at the time, when one day he invited me to go with Keshub and others to Dakshineswar. Of course I, too, was eager to see with mine own eyes what sort of a holy man Rama Krishna was.

"On our arrival at the Kali temple, we found a very strange-looking man whose eyes were like a hawk's. They saw and recognised your worth at a great distance. The only thing I remember of that interview is this. Just as we were getting ready to take our leave, the Master said, 'Keshub, though you lecture a great deal your fame will not reach very far. But this lad,' he pointed at Vivekananda, 'will be famous across the seas.' Everyone present laughed at Rama Krishna's remark. We thought he was making fun of the fame and fortune which Keshub had won. But about a decade later when I read the reports of Vivekananda's lectures in England

and America, I often thought of what the Holy One had said of him at their first meeting."

That prophecy of Rama Krishna's instead of pleasing Vivekananda offended him. For to him, at the time, it sounded like officiousness and fakery. He hated palmists, fortune-tellers, sybils and soothsayers. However, in spite of the strong dislike that he had for the Master, he felt drawn to the latter more and more strongly as day succeeded day. Something within him prodded his obstinate intellect to give the holy man another chance. At last with the desire to find out for the second and the last time what sort Rama Krishna was, Vivekananda called on him once more. During his journey to Dakshineswar he felt disturbed. He said to himself: "Why am I going to see this fool of God? I know God does not exist. Then why do I go? . . ." So on all the way!

On his arrival in Dakshineswar he found Rama Krishna sitting on his couch, all alone. That relieved Vivekananda. He said to himself, "Now he will not embarrass me by making silly prophecies about my future in the presence of a crowd."

Hardly had Vivekananda said those words to himself when the Master irritated him anew with his words of greeting: "I am so glad you have come. I have waited for you many years."

With an expression of chill effrontery on his face Vivekananda sat on the edge of the couch. For a while neither of them spoke a word. One can imagine those two faces studying each other. The Master looked old. He was old beyond his age, while the youth before him had a face massive and strong as a "young Buddha of Bronze."

The latter panoplied with beauty and youth, and the former destitute of everything save the invisible God sat scrutinising each other. Suddenly without a word, without the slightest sound, Rama Krishna lifted his right foot, slowly moved it forward and brought it into contact with Vivekananda's body. No sooner had that happened than . . .

"That instant," said Vivekananda, "before my wide-open eyes the walls of the room reeled and fell; then the furniture possessed by some demoniac force dashed itself on the floor, then sank into a void. All around me was Nothing, Nothing! And suddenly the lean-mouthed Universe set to devour my 'Meness.' Then I thought to myself. 'To lose one's ego is to die!' Death was so near that I could touch it! Frightened by that sinister realisation I shrieked for help: 'Oh! you! What are you doing to me? I want to live. Do not let me die yet, for my father and my mother are living.' At those words of mine, that Madman laughed aloud; gently rubbed my chest with his hand, and added: 'Let us stop now; it is not necessary to see it all in one flash. Later you shall know the rest.' After these words, as if by a wizardry, the furniture, walls, the room and myself all arrranged themselves as before.

"Later that day I wondered if it was hypnotism or mesmerism that had been practised on me. The very fact that none of the events of my latest experience squared with the symptoms of either, left me all the more troubled. I came to no conclusion save that there are hidden mysteries about and beyond us that our intellectual insolence can never uncover. That experience of mine convinced me that Rama Krishna was not mad. A madman cannot pulverise into dust one's senses and intellect. Thinking and cogitating about my experience I spent the rest of the day with him hoping that he would throw some more light on it. At last the sun set, and since I had to get home soon, I bowed to his feet, then rose to depart. But Rama Krishna would not let me go without extracting from me the promise that I would come to see him soon again."

Vivekananda was in no haste to see him again though his heart yearned for it. He spent many days thinking over his recent experience. It fascinated as well as frightened him.

No matter from what standpoint he examined it, he could not find a satisfactory explanation of it. And to crown all his perplexities a voice within his soul said: "Go to him. He alone can make it clear." As time passed, that cry grew more and more insistent. Nothing could still it. At last like a river to the sea, he obeyed the urge of his soul, and called on *Shree* Rama Krishna again.

"The third visit that I paid Him," says Vivekananda, "proved most startling. On my arrival I found Him strolling in the garden.

"He asked me to join him. From the garden we sauntered to the river bank. Thence walking in a leisurely fashion we went indoors. He sat on his couch and I seated myself on its edge as I had done before. Just then he touched me again. This time . . ."

Vivekananda never divulged the contents of his last experience. What happened then may have meant too much to him. It was not to be profaned by being told, at least by himself. But years later Brahmananda, "M," and Saradananda—all three—asked Rama Krishna about it. And the Master explained: "When Vivekananda lost his temporal 'I,' I asked him some questions about himself. I questioned him particularly about the full amount of realisations that he had already accomplished. Why had he come to earth? He gave me answers that were clear. And they brought me certainty; for all those things I had known about him in my meditation. All the same it was good to get his verification. I concluded this also, that the very next time if in meditation he comes upon the exact story of his Self he will at once spit away his body and soar back to his Home. For he is a fully realised Soul."

About nineteen years later, when Vivekananda died in the Monastery, he died in the supreme meditation that had gone on about three days. This happened seventeen years after the death of Rama Krishna. I have seen the room where Vivekananda meditated; also I have interviewed those who kept constant watch on him during those days. They told me what the elder holy men heard Rama Krishna speak of years before.

After his latest experience Vivekananda gradually drew nearer the Master, and took lessons in meditation and other practices. Even then he hesitated to renounce the world and take the vow of a Sanyasin—mendicant holy man. Time and again he said to Rama Krishna: "Please tell the Divine Mother to provide for my family so that I can take the begging bowl." Rama Krishna answered: "I can not. *You* go and pray to Her."

Bhupendranath Basu, who has been quoted already, tells a story that explains one of Vivekananda's hesitations. "Every now and then," says Basu, "Vivekananda would vanish from the lawyer's office where he and I were working at the time. Sometimes our employer sent me searching after the truant. I went to Rama Krishna's place and many other haunts of his but never could find him anywhere. At last one day I asked him about his doings. He vouchsafed me no answer. But God-quest, like murder, generally gets found out. One day after I had left our law office I walked home through another part of the town. This was a dangerous slum district; not a single member of our caste deliberately went there. There, as I was going along, taking in with each glance the terrible poverty of the people, lo! suddenly, I saw a man in ocher-colored robe begging at the door of a filthy hovel. I could not believe my eyes. How could these destitute people give alms to anybody? And what kind of a beggar is it that begs of the lowest? As I drew near I noticed that the Sanyasin was blessing the poor old woman who had given him a handful of rice. Then as he turned to go I saw his face. It was Vivekananda. Now that we were face to face he asked me to follow him. We walked briskly away, and in a short time reached the river bank where we sat down on the upper steps of a Ghaut. Vivekananda said 'You can see that my dress explains everything. I want to be a Sanyasin. Rama Krishna draws me so that I would consider it Heaven if I could enter his order to-morrow. But I am not sure of myself. I do not wish to offer him a weak character. It is not easy to be a monk. You know our family—its prestige of caste and wealth. Though we are poor now, we were not so twenty years ago. A great deal is expected of us. I feel terribly proud. It is my pride that stands in my way. Can I, my father's son, become as humble as a Sanyasin? Can I sink my pride so that I can live by begging? In order to find all that out I put on the monk's garb and beg in the slums. I get very little from them materially speaking. But spiritually what they are giving me is more than abundant—they are enabling me to lose my pride. I feel very humble now. Probably I shall be able to renounce all and become a worthy disciple of my Guru.

" 'Another thing I have found out that gives me courage is that I can go without food for a number of days. Not only is my mind free of pride, but my body can stand starvation. I feel that I can ask Rama Krishna to give me initiation. I have already mastered the science of meditation, and can perform all the austerities of yoga. But I have not dared to ask for the final initiation until I have made quite sure of myself.' "

Now that he had conquered his own weaknesses Vivekananda was tormented by the problem of providing for his family. In spite of many discussions between him and Rama Krishna, neither of them prayed to the Mother. Apparently they did not wish to ask God to provide for his family. Here again Vivekananda's pride stood in his way: though he could beg from men, he could not beg of God.

One day he took up the matter with his own mother. That austere and proud lady brought up in the strictest discipline of the *ancien régime* said to her boy: "Since when did a member of our family give up God for the fear of poverty? Your own grandfather renounced wife, children, wealth and position the moment he heard the Secret of secrets knock at the door of his heart. Did I not pray to God long before you were born that you should be a man of religion? Now that the Infinite stands at the gates of your life, you want to turn Him away! None of your ancestors would have done such a thing. What right have you to be afraid of poverty for me?"

Vivekananda bowed his head and walked towards Dakshineswar determined to end all his troubles by taking initiation from his Guru. But on his way he cogitated: "I must provide for my dependents. Brave ancestors are all very good. But am I my ancestor?

No, until Rama Krishna says that my family are provided for, I shall let God alone." Thus soliloquizing he tramped the road. All this while his longing to receive the full and final illumination from his Master was growing so that it became irresistible. So by the time he had reached the Holy One's presence, he was a man of decided will.

Rama Krishna apparently had sensed all that, so he said sweetly: "The Lord is stronger than any one of us. What have you allowed to trouble your thoughts?"

Vivekananda answered with vehemence: "My Lord, I must renounce the world. But the hungry for whom I am responsible must be guaranteed security from starvation. Will you not speak to the Divine Mother?"

Rama Krishna said: "I will not disturb Her with such trivialities. But I say that your dependents will never lack necessities." That boon from the Master cleared the last obstacle from the path of his initiation.

Now he was initiated and given the name Vivekananda. For that was not the name his parents gave him. They called him Narendra. The names that are given to newly initiated holy men are found in meditation by their Masters. They are not of haphazard choice. Vivekananda's name means the bliss of discrimination. Why was he given that? As a youth he was so kind that he wanted others to enjoy the same benefits from Rama Krishna as himself. He used to bring all sorts of people to the Holy One and urged the Master to afford them the "Beatific Vision." Rama Krishna used to wail with patient suffering: "How can I give every waif this Vision when they do not bring it with them? Why do you not use your discrimination?" No doubt Vivekananda was a man of discrimination in his mind and soul. It was his heart that needed to be purged of sentimentality. It was during those four or five years of his training before his initiation, that his heart, though tender as ever, grew keen with discrimination. And when he was initiated the name that was revealed to him by his Guru was Vivekananda—discrimination that is bliss. For the last time the Holy One enjoined him against sentimentality:

"Do three things in conduct. Never lose your taste for God. Respect all sincere devotees of God, no matter where or when. And do not try to be sentimentally kind to others—You, brother-in-law (idiot), smaller than an insect, how dare you humiliate one of His creatures by your pity. The thing that you must do is to see and serve each living being as the Absolute God." That was Rama Krishna's Golden Rule.

"See and serve every living being as the Absolute God."

After his initiation Vivekananda had to work much harder than before. He had to practise and master still higher concentration —a science that only an initiate can explain. Fortunately he has left us some of its results in his commentaries on Raja yoga, a book quite well known in America.

After he had studied and mastered all that Rama Krishna had to teach, Vivekananda was sent on a pilgrimage to many yogis who lived scattered all over India. It was during this voyage of discovery that the young initiate met Pavahari (the Air-eater), one of the greatest teachers of Yoga in modern times. The Air-eater simply charmed Vivekananda, for he was a virtuoso of Yoga. He could do all that Rama Krishna did: no doubt Vivekananda was glad to get a verification of his own Master's authentic powers from another source. He stayed a long time with the Air-eater. But in the end he found the great yogi wanting in one respect. Despite all his powers, Pavahari lacked compassion. He was not willing to live in this world of weak and suffering men in order to help them. He did not believe that other human beings needed his help. He said: "When they need my help they will come to my cave on the mountain top. I will not go down to live in the market-place in order to teach them. If they want to be lions, men must go and live in the desert."

That sentence opened Vivekananda's eyes. He saw at once that the Air-eater was not an absolute Guru. Pavahari had not attained to the spiritual stature of Rama Krishna. No sooner had he realised that than he left the Air-eater's cave. He came to Dakshineswar and gave a full report of his year's pilgrimage to Rama Krishna. He asked him: "Why does the Air-eater hoard his knowledge in a mountain cave? Why does he not squander all he has upon the world as you do?"

Rama Krishna smiled at his ingenuous disciple. "But I hoard it here. I do not go to many places preaching. Do I?"

"No. But you are so eager to give help. And you live here where everyone can see you."

The Master explained: "The Air-eater has more regard for the purity in which knowledge of God should be kept. It should be guarded from the profane and the ignorant. His taste is good. But I am without taste."

"There must be a deeper reason than that," said Vivekananda. But Rama Krishna smiled again, and refused to talk.

Now that he had traveled and studied all that the other teachers of India had to offer, Vivekananda was ripe for the next stage of his development. After teaching him some more, Rama Krishna said: "Now debate with all the scholars and yogis who come to see me.

Test what you have been taught by pitting it against what they know. You have got the gold, now put it through the fire of criticism."

Day after day Vivekananda met in fierce mental contest pundits and holy men who came to Dakshineswar. All of their debates were carried on in Sanskrit. And the chief rule that the contestants followed was that every quotation that anyone made should be correct and from memory. No one was allowed to quote from a printed page.

It was after his success as an intellectual debator had been thoroughly established that one of the visitors urged Rama Krishna to put an end to such nonsense. He said: "What can your disciples gain by humbling other men's intellect? Take the case of young Vivekananda; he never loses a debate. Some of these days he will grow conceited and quarrelsome like a serpent raising his head at everybody."

Rama Krishna answered: "He is building up his mental muscles during these exercises. He will have to wrestle with the pundits of distant lands after I am gone. I must see to it now that he is properly trained and equipped. As for conceit, he is a realised Soul, it will never touch him. He is not unripe."

Soon afterwards Rama Krishna sent Vivekananda on his second pilgrimage. This time he crossed both the length and breadth of India. There is hardly a district that he did not visit. Wherever there was a railway line he went by train. But to points that were beyond he journeyed on foot.

Vivekananda was averse to going on his second pilgrimage. He prayed Rama Krishna: "I do not wish to wander. I want to be near you. It is you whom I love. From you I have obtained my salvation; from you I have learnt all that is worth while. Oh! please, do not send me away. Let me stay near and learn from you."

"But you must," answered the Guru firmly. "You must go and visit the common people's homes. For they live by a secret that never dies. Soon after my death a day will come when you will have to preach to multitudes far and near. At that hour you will find the result of all this. Through your voice will be heard the clamor of a thousand spiritual realisations."

Again, with a blessing on his lips and a begging bowl between his hands, Vivekananda set forth on his pilgrimage, this time "to learn from the lowest of the lowly and those who are lost altogether—and holy."

Though Vivekananda traveled unknown—for who would care to know the name of a holy man—yet he left indelible marks of his personality on many minds. "Very few failed to feel the presence of that stallion of spirituality foaled by father Rama Krishna."

The late Mahratta Sanskrit scholar and patriot, Tilak, once met him in a train. Tilak says: "I saw him sitting on the seat next to myself. He looked like a Buddha. But I despised mendicants, no matter what they looked like. In order to amuse myself by humiliating him I decided to talk to this ignorant faker on metaphysics in Sanskrit. For I was sure that philosophy he had never heard of, and as for Sanskrit . . . So I began. To my astonishment he answered me in the language of the Gods. But that was not enough to convince me of anything, so I started a discussion of Vedanta with him. As our debate progressed I was struck more and more by two things; the lucidity of his mind and the dignity of his style. When the train reached my town, Poona, I invited him to come and stay in my house. Though he spent a week with us I never asked him for his name. After all, why bother a man who has renounced the world with such a worldly thing? About ten years after he left me I read in the newspapers the cabled reports of some lectures on Vedanta given in America by one Vivekananda. After reading and re-reading several quotations from his speech, I said to myself, 'It is my young holy man. It bears the stamp of his mind.' Then on his return to India I met him again. Of course it was Vivekananda."

Whatever success the "young holy man" won, we know now, was already anticipated by Rama Krishna. The very best that came out of Vivekananda was what he acquired, as he himself admits, at his Master's feet. "If

I have said anything that is original, noble and good, I owe it to Him. And if you ask me about the price I like to pay for knowing Him: if there is a Hell, I am willing to live there three thousand years for every year that I spent in the company of Shree Rama Krishna."

When Vivekananda returned from his second long pilgrimage the Master remarked: "Now that you have suffered the hardships of deserts and jungles, and now that you have seen almost all there is to see, stay by me. Help me to train and bless all who come here. We must soon finish our joint work, for the time is fast approaching for me to go."

CHAPTER IX

RAMA KRISHNA AND HIS DISCIPLES (*Continued*)

I HAVE already intimated that one of the most important disciples of Rama Krishna, Turyananda, died recently in Benares. I had the privilege of being with him before his death. Since he was quite aware of his approaching end, Swami Turyananda did his utmost to tell people everything that he knew of Yoga, Vedanta and Shree Rama Krishna. Though a very reticent man, at the moment he spoke without any reserve. Because he traveled very little, those who wished to see him had to go to the Benares Monastery where he lived. In the Monastery as well as all over the holy city people used to call the Swami—Kesari, the maned one. His face so full of compassion was also grim as a lion's: not an atom of superfluous flesh, not a single line of worry. Wherever he went, people knew him as a son of God. One day another young man and I took a walk with him. He walked a little ahead, while we followed at a distance of half a dozen yards. In a few minutes a peasant came by. He stared at the holy man as they passed each other. Then when he saw us and also noticed in our gaze that we had remarked his staring at the "Maned One," he stopped short and asked, "Who is that man ahead of you?" We questioned him: "Why do you ask?" The peasant paused a moment, then said: "No man can hold his head so high as yon man. Even a King cannot hold his head thus, nor a merchant prince. Only the son of the Real King holds his head so high. He is a Brahmajnanin!" Such was the majesty of Swami Turyananda. It was purely spiritual. That is why it communicated itself without any effort even to the commonest peasant.

It was one of the common folk who told me of Turyananda's early life. He was born, I learnt, in an orthodox Brahmin family of Bengal. His father, who was one of the ablest

Sanskrit scholars of his time, trained the boy in Vedanta and Yoga. Before he had passed his teens, Turyananda knew Patanjali yoga by heart. As for the Mimangsa philosophy he knew both the Purva and the Uttara so well that he used to take over his father's class any time that gentleman happened to be away from home. As for the Upanishads and the Shankara Vasya, even in his old age I heard him recite and explain chapter and verse from memory for more than two hours at a stretch. He amazed groups of Pundits who came to consult him, not only by the accuracy of his quotations but also with the ravishing clarity of his interpretation. Once someone asked him: "Where did you acquire so much knowledge and such powers of convincing people?"

The Maned One replied: "My father taught me almost all of it, and Shree Rama Krishna fulfilled the rest."

From childhood on, Turyananda showed such a religious zeal that his entire family expected him to be a holy man. So one day in his twentieth year when he came home and announced to his family that he had found his Guru, no one was surprised. He said further: "This afternoon some class-mates of mine took me to Dakshineswar to see Rama Krishna. As usual the Master was surrounded by a group of listeners. I had to wait till those who had come before me finished questioning him. However, when my turn came I asked the Master 'Can any man know God?' He answered 'If God is willing.'

"That answer of Rama Krishna's set me thinking. Why is it that all the men of the past who had seen God said the same thing? For instance, Shankara who was proud to the verge of insolence said after his realization: 'I am a part of Thee, and through Thy compassion I can be one with Thee.' The same way spoke Chaitanya and others. At present Rama Krishna proclaims the self-same Truth. I have studied and practised Yoga to the utmost. But that will not suffice. Now I must go to Dakshineswar to be trained by him in the art of rousing God's compassion."

After his first interview, encouraged by his family, Turyananda paid some further visits to Rama Krishna. It was during one of those visits that he met Vivekananda. Soon they became deeply attached to each other. From now on they studied many ancient Sanskrit works together. Whether it was in the Upanishads or the Yoga texts whenever they failed to understand anything they went to Rama Krishna for elucidation, for his were the only answers that satisfied them completely. One day when he had solved a very difficult problem raised in a text they exclaimed: "Sir, you who never read these books, how do you know what they mean?"

Rama Krishna answered: "I belong to the Great House. The place that I have been to, your books have not yet reached."

On another occasion he remarked: "If you know the Creator, His creation is automatically caught like a fish in the net of your knowledge."

Blessed and thrilled by the words and companionship of Rama Krishna, Vivekananda said to Turyananda as they were walking home, "Tell me what you think of the Master." Turyananda answered: "I cannot begin to tell. But let me quote the ancient Sanskrit:

"If the Himalayas were an inkwell,
And the Ocean itself was the ink,
Then if the endless forests gave all their leaves
For the Muse herself to write,
Yet her lightning pen
Could not begin to describe His Glory."

Through Turyananda one got an indication of the spiritual stature of Rama Krishna. There is no doubt that Turyananda was one of the universally accepted holy men of our time. He spoke very little, but when he gave his opinion it was in no uncertain terms. I have heard him speak of Rama Krishna with the awe and worship that other men give to God.

Within several years of his first visit to Rama Krishna, Turyananda took the begging bowl and became a novice, a Brahmachari, and soon afterwards was given Sannyas, initiation. Then it was that his name Hari was given up, and Rama Krishna named him Turyananda. Turya is a difficult word to translate. It is a cosmic state next to the final identity with God. Anyone who has attained this state can cross over and realise Samadhi,

Identity, at will. Since we shall return to the life-work of Turyananda in a later chapter, I would now speak of that unique disciple of Rama Krishna whose name was Lattu Maharaj.

I have already said that Turyananda was a scholar. But his contempt for scholarship without realisation of God was boundless. And his admiration for realisation without any scholarship was passionate. That is why he held such a high opinion about Lattu who was an untutored young servant of a merchant prince from the West Country. It was in the company of his rich employer that Lattu came East on pilgrimage. While passing through Calcutta that merchant, in order to acquire merit, did all the charities enjoined by his religion. But as if that was not enough, he said: "Is there no other thing that I can do in order to acquire further merit?" He repeated this question to men and women he met. At last in sheer exasperation someone of his servants informed him, "There is a holy man in Dakshineswar to whom you have not paid homage."

So the next day the merchant and his servants set out for Dakshineswar. They went up the river in the most gorgeous boats; one can visualize the scene: the gold-turbaned merchant in pure white tunic of pilgrimage, his white beard combed and perfumed, his dark eyes keenly watching all things and all men from his boat whose turquoise sails blown by the southern wind pulled over the tawny waters. Behind him followed his servants dressed in purple and blue and red seated in three other white boats, one of which contained Lattu who held a plate of solid gold covered with gems. This was the offering to be made to the Holy One. At the moment little did he realise that the Master wanted his soul and nothing less. As they went up the river against green banks that glowed like emerald aflame in the hot morning sun, they passed bathers performing their morning ablutions, and swiftly moving barges laden with fruits piled up pyramid fashion. Mountains of oranges and mangoes gleamed under bellying sails of the color of jade.

At last they reached Dakshineswar. They

went up the spacious granite steps of the Ghaut like jeweled insects crawling up the side of a giant structure. On reaching the top they turned to the left away from the shrine of the Mother. The goddess was secondary to them to-day. They wanted to see Him, the Living Teacher. They walked towards the garden. After they had gone a hundred yards or so, they heard through the open doorway of a room the low but resonant voice of the Master. The sound of it was unmistakable. They waited till he finished talking. Now there was silence within. So they ventured to enter, the merchant first and Lattu following with the offering plate of gold. There in the cool darkness of the room they felt refreshed. They waited and watched. At last their eyes grew accustomed to the shadowy atmosphere. Now they could see. A tall old man, not attractive looking, was seated on a long couch leaning against a snow-white pillow. His clothes were almost fallen away from his body. But he was not aware of it. Near at his feet sat shaven-headed men wrapped in attention. Nobody said a word at the intrusion of the strangers. The merchant bowed and made some appropriate remarks. Then Lattu walked forward and put the offering at the Master's feet. The precious stones gleamed at him, but Rama Krishna saw none of them. Lo! his gaze was fixed on Lattu's face. That face—long expected—was there in its utter innocence. Lattu did not yet know what had happened. As soon as the day's ceremony was over, he and his master went away to sell the gems and the gold plate in order to give their proceeds to the poor. For that is what the Master had commanded them to do.

In two days Lattu was back. Rama Krishna was discoursing, seated on his couch in the same room, and about half a dozen of his disciples were listening to his talk. The moment Lattu entered the room the Master stood up, tall as a tree, saying: "Why? Why do you come back?"

Lattu, with tears streaming down his cheeks, said: "I missed you, Lord, in the past, but in this incarnation do not let me lose you." Then he fell and buried his face between the feet of the Master. Lattu's conversion was immediate, spontaneous. He had no storm and stress of book-learning to go through. As Turyananda is reported to have said: "Many of us waded through the mirky waters of scholarship, toiling laboriously against the tides of conceit in order to cross over to the other side where the Lord was. But this fellow, Lattu, like Hanuman the Monkey, leaped over all that and in one bound reached the feet of Mukti (salvation). What insight! What spiritual certainty! Oh! Lattu was the superior of all of us. He reached his Master unsoiled by the conceit of scholarship and unscarred by the cutting current of doubt."

After Rama Krishna's death, Lattu lived in the Math (Monastery) in Benares during the latter part of his life. He lived very near Turyananda. In this place there is a hospital where the poor sick people are taken care of by the monks and the nuns.

But Lattu was suspicious of doing good. He had a feeling that if men and women did good without attaining insight into the secret of Life they were being caught in a routine from which no authentic good could accrue. One day a conceited young fellow said: "I agree with you—doing good is a snare." Lattu answered "But holy men like Turyananda and Vivekananda have fallen into it. That means it is a snare worth being caught in."

Lattu was convinced that we do good by becoming all the Goodness of God. He did not believe in healing through prayers. He always went to a doctor when he was sick, and had no morbid love of pain. But at last one day, walking bare-footed, he was scratched by a piece of sharp tin lying on the road. He limped his way home to the monastery and went to the hut of Turyananda. "Well," he said, "I hear the flute playing at last. I must go to the tryst with Him."

Turyananda, when he saw the wounded foot, at once sent for a doctor and put Lattu to bed. "But," Lattu repeated, "it is no use this time. I hear Him fluting for me. The doctor cannot prevent my keeping that tryst." In spite of all the efforts the doctors made, gangrene set in. Within a fortnight Lattu had walked "between rivers of Light and reached the Homeland of his Beloved."

Thus ends the story of Rama Krishna's unscholarly disciple. He went into meditation and stayed in Samadhi the last four days of his illness. He never lost consciousness. "Until he spat away his body," as the monks say, "he remained in complete Identity."

CHAPTER X

DESCRIPTION OF THE INDESCRIBABLE

THE reader may ask, "What did Rama Krishna mean by 'Seeing God'? What does Samadhi mean? What are the stages of development through which one attains the state of Samadhi?"

During my course of gathering the Rama Krishna legends it became more and more necessary to learn of the nature of the spiritual experience that held his disciples to his side. "Why is it that such strong healthy young persons never wearied of him? What made them stay near him with so much devotion? What wonders did he show them? How came they to be blind to the attractions of this world? Did Rama Krishna offer them a greater and deeper attraction?"

All those questions I put before Swami Turyananda in Benares. He said in answer: "Rama Krishna showed us the Face of the Eternal. After that we stayed on with him hoping that through his compassion and by training, we would see Him again. Once a disciple always a disciple. Think of the possibility of being thrown in Samadhi—a thing for which men toil a hundred incarnations—by one single touch of his finger or foot! How could we leave his side, we who were so greedy like all youth to taste Bliss Absolute again and again. He enabled us to stare into the Eyes of God at least once; that naturally blinded us to this world. We see nothing here, and whatever we do see is filled with the brimming Light of TAT (That). No matter what we see or feel it says, 'You are He, you are He.—*Tat Tam asi.*' That is what Rama Krishna did to us. After such an event we were tethered to him as the bird is to the sky—it may go very far in many directions, yet it will remain under the many-branched sky."

It is a well-known fact that his chelas often

pressed Rama Krishna to describe the indedescribable. But even he maintained: "God-consciousness cannot be explained through words. Only experience, not phrases, can reveal to you the full magnitude of the Invisible."

But in spite of that the devoted group of disciples urged him to speak particularly of his own experience of Samadhi, Oneness, with the Absolute, Brahman.

Rama Krishna asked to be excused. "I cannot see why I should explain it to you whom I have trained and helped to attain that experience. If it can be put into words why do you not do it?"

"But, my Lord," the disciples said, "we cannot live in it as long as you can. You who have stayed in Samadhi six, seven days at a time are the one to explain it. In the presence of Silence how dare we speak?" But Rama Krishna only smiled at their bare-faced compliment. Then a very keen-witted young man tried another way of making him speak. "But, my Lord, how do we know that every one of us attains the same experience, when our paths are different. For instance, when I meditate and quicken all my being with the thought of Oneness, my spiritual energy does not act the same way as that of another."

"Ah, that is a comparison of the way men's intuition acts," replied the Master. "That is easy to describe. Here," meaning himself, "I experimented on all the ways in order to verify them. But no matter how my spiritual energy acted at the end it rose to the seventh valley and there I beheld . . ."

That instant Rama Krishna passed into Samadhi. His breathing stopped. His heart ceased working. And his pulse beat no more. Were it not for the even temperature of his body there was no way of distinguishing him from a corpse. Of course there was nothing alarming about it; his apostles had seen him in that state very often, days at a time. At last when he came out of Samadhi he resumed his discourse:

"Oh, my sons, I try to explain it to you. But the experience is so great words cannot render it. You must plunge yourself into the waters of that experience. For there is no other way of fathoming it. Your mind and intellect, swift though they are, cannot overtake the lightning-steed of God-consciousness. Those two only raise the dust of words in which they get lost."

"But, my Lord, you said that the ways in which the soul-sight (Dharma-eye) rises in a man you can explain."

"Yes," agreed Rama Krishna. "Though what the Dharma-eye sees is indescribable, yet the paths it travels are within the reach of words. And though the end is the same, yet the ways of reaching it are diverse. The Rishis (sages) of old have enumerated at least five different ways that the soul-energy of men rises to God when they kindle themselves with prayers and meditation. For instance sometimes a man's soul-power moves, as the Rishis say, like the hop, hop, hop of a toad. Sometimes it runs as a snake glides up a hillside, in flashes and curves. Then there is still another way. Each cell of your body and every pulse of your heart beat slowly; the regularity of the rhythm with which your intuitions catch fire is slow and inevitable as the march of a row of ants from one food-center to another. The fourth way is the way of a bird or birds. You know how birds fly off one tree and move in the air, as though they were wandering aimlessly. Yet they alight on a distant tree that has been in their mind all the while. Similarly rises and alights on the Divine your soul-energy when thoroughly quickened by persistent devotion. Each atom of your being seems to fly up on the wings of all-piercing Light. It may wander about aimlessly at first. But if you keep on meditating and praying those wings will bring you to the House of Oneness.

"The fifth way is quite different from the others. The sages have called it the Way of Monkeys. You can sometimes see monkeys sitting still like a rock. Then suddenly they start leaping and bounding, and they do not stop until they have reached their destination—somebody's mango garden. So acts your spiritual sight. You sit still and meditate day after day, yet nothing happens. But you keep on thinking of Oneness with your body, heart, mind, and soul. Let not even a particle of you flag, concentrate hard till in the course of two or three years suddenly your Insight leaps from plane to plane, scaling the steepest precipices with the ease of a hawk, then plunges into Advaita—Oneness with Infinite Intelligence."

Now Rama Krishna closed his eyes and sat still. Slowly he passed into Samadhi. Again his listeners had to wait a long time. It may sound incredible but the patience with which they waited on their Master surpasses all measurement. On this occasion nearly an hour had passed when Rama Krishna came out of Samadhi and resumed his discourse.

"Next to the difference of the ways a Soul climbs to Oneness you must watch for the planes of consciousness that you must traverse. No matter whose meditation—whether of Lord Buddha or of a common man—it must take him across six different valleys, planes of consciousness, in order to reach the seventh, the last. Whether your Soul's intuition hops like a toad or flies like a bird, it must behold the seven valleys."

"Is the experience of each one of those valleys the same, no matter how a soul reaches it?" asked one of the disciples.

"Yes," answered the Master. "It is identically the same."

The same disciple asked him further: "And did you commence your meditation the same way every time? Was your method at all different from what we do?"

Rama Krishna: "There is no difference at all between them. I sat still, as my Guru advised me, and purified my thoughts and feelings of all the dross of separation. In my mind, in my heart, in my soul, in every cell of my body I sought His Presence. I knew that I was not separate from Him. He was in ME. Hence I quickened every bit of myself to elicit the hidden Self. 'Come forth, O thou sword of immortality, from this thy scabbard.' Thus I prayed; days, weeks, and months. At last my Insight hopped—hop, hop, hop . . . it leaped over the embankment of this world into the waters of the first of the seven valleys. A light utterly unknown, like another sun, shone upon what I perceived. All the things of this earth that I looked upon wore the vesture of Beauty. Everywhere I glanced, beyond and around, beauty and spirituality leaped out of matter like tigers from dark dens. Now I was aware that this was the home of the senses. The sight of so much wonder filled me with terrible appetites. 'Possess, possess,' they cried. I was seized with an overpowering desire to taste and own all the beauty that lay about me. Just at that moment another cry broke out in me: 'Beware, beware of the sinister temptation of this valley!'

"No sooner heard than done. I set out to quicken my meditation. I meditated harder and prayed more intensely for release from the first valley. At the end of some months my prayers were answered. The world of the senses tempted me no more: slowly the first valley fell from my consciousness as the skeleton of its prey falls from the eagle's talons."

Now that Rama Krishna had taken the best out of it, he left the first valley behind.

"I had entered the second valley. Here I was not obsessed with the clawing material beauty of what I saw. The light in which the world appeared now was more refined, more subtle, and soothing. I felt happy here. Fragments of beautiful colors, shapes, and sounds haunted and sweetened my hours in this valley. I thought of relaxing my meditation and staying here. Just then I was tempted to create life: 'Things of Sex.' For in the sublime light of the second valley, sex wears the appearance of beatitude and power. But no matter how it appears, the soul must resist its temptation. I set out to free my consciousness from the besetting beauty of sex. I heaped more fuel of devotion on the altar of God-quest. The fire of Illumination burnt very low at first. But gradually it became brighter. And in a few more days, lo, it burnt like daggers of light. And in those biting flames the second valley burnt into cinders. Neither it nor its temptations fretted me further.

"Thus I reached the third stage. In this valley I found that the sense of power that I had experienced before, in the second, had increased a hundredfold. Now I felt that I could take the sun between the palms of my hands and crush it into a handful of burning dust. This sense of power must be resisted. It is nothing but a test of one's character. There is no temptation viler than the sense of power. The instant I had perceived the danger that beset me, I quickened my meditation to the utmost. It had to be more powerful than the power that I had to resist. I prayed —oh! how I prayed—to be free of my sense of power. Like the fangs of a viper it held me. But my soul would not yield to it. I rose on the wings of meditation higher and higher till height had no meaning for me. At that moment the serpent opened its mouth and fell from my side!

"Now like an elephant hurtling through a fence I plunged on the valley of (Hridaya Jyoti) the Light of God's Heart. As if my heart had become a torch lit by the flame from His, light fell from my soul over everything. Pebbles and stars—all sang with equal radiance a song of the Ineffable. In this fourth valley I felt wellnigh secure from every temptation. Yet I kept a strict watch on myself. Though I was a chalice of light, yet I felt suspicious . . . of temptation. That feeling served me as a warning. I decided not to tarry here. Thus followed another long period of fasting, prayer, and meditation.

"Fortunately this time I did not have to wait so very long. The light in my heart expanded. It flung a vast circle like a net of suns around and beyond. And lo! I had reached the next valley, the realm of Utterance. My thoughts and feelings, every pulse and each cell of me was illumined! Through my throat and lips poured words of wonder and Benediction. I praised the Lord all the time. Save of Him I could not bear to speak. And if anyone spoke of possessions and pleasures, their words smote me like rods. It got to be so that if any of my relatives came to consult me on family matters I used to run away and hide myself in the woods of Panchabati. Relations or friends who sought to own me appeared to me as a deep well dragging me down—I feared to be suffocated in the water way below in the dark earth. I felt as though drowning in their presence. Only by leaving them could I find peace. In one word: this valley is not full of tolerance and love for all. One must transcend it.

"That is why I flung myself into deeper and steeper meditations yet. There was no peace nor pleasure for me. 'Either find Him face to face or take my life,' I counseled myself. As a tiger crouches in order to leap, so did I. I prayed, I waited, I watched. I would not linger in the valley of utterance; I must not give in to merely praising God. I must see Him. So I sat couchant with prayers. Suddenly I perceived something ahead. That instant I leaped—In a trice I was in the sixth, the valley of Turya. Here I was close to my Beloved. I could see and feel Him in the next chamber. Only a thin transparent veil separated the soul from the self. At last I knew that I was in a room in the House of Oneness.

"From the sixth valley it is not difficult to pass on to the seventh. There no word can enter, nor the chatter of human thought. Only your soul clad in Silence can lift the veil that separates Him from your embrace."

A long silence fell after Rama Krishna had

finished speaking. But instead of meditating the rest of the day on what the Master had said, one of the young men questioned: "People say that you are ignorant, my Lord, yet how do you know all that the sages of the past wrote? For what you have told us lies buried in tomes of metaphysics. I am told you are an ignorant man."

Rama Krishna answered in a way quite different from his usual answer, "I never studied profound books, but I have heard scholars discuss them. Having heard—and gathering what rang true for my own needs—I made a garland of them and put them around my neck. Then I flung every inch of it at the feet of God saying, 'Mother, take all your erudite tomes and laws. All I want is love of Thee!'"

Just at that moment someone raised a very significant question: "My Lord, all that you have told us is pleasing to the soul and satisfying to the heart. But my wayward mind wishes to know this: he who starts his meditation with desire of Oneness has to do so by saying, feeling and realising—'I am He, I am

He!' But what about those who start the opposite way, saying: 'Thou art not me yet I seek Thee!' What happens to them, my Lord? Do they too cross those valleys and become One with Him? Or, do they remain separate from Him for ever?"

Rama Krishna answered without any pause or hesitation: "That is about ultimate matters. But there is no difference: whether you call Him 'Thou' or call Him 'I am He.' Men that realise Him through 'Thou' have a very lovely relation with Him. It is very much like that of an old trusted servant with his Master. As they both grow old, the Master leans and depends on his friend the servant more and more. Towards the end of his life the Master consults his pearl of a servant regarding every serious matter that he wishes to undertake. One day, deeply pleased with his servitor's devotion, the Master takes him by the hand, then seats him on his own august seat. The servant is embarrassed, and in his excitement says, 'What are you doing, my Lord?' But the Master holds him on the throne next to Himself saying, 'You are the same as I, my Beloved.' So, though we worship God as one apart, yet if we worship Him with sincerity and consecration, He will some day very suddenly makes us one with Himself. That is Samadhi."

There is a legend that at one time some friends of Rama Krishna urged him to explain Samadhi. They said: "If you say something about it you prove everything. Give us a definition of Samadhi, and that will give us a definition of God."

But the wary Holy One replied: "And if I give you a definition of God, what will you do with it? Oh, I know what you will eventually do; you will make a creed of it in order to found a new religion in my name. I did not come to earth to start another cult. Oh, no!"

However, it is reported that on another occasion Rama Krishna incidentally defined God. Some visitors asked him: "Will you please resolve what seems to us a contradiction? People say that you have attained Identity: you are He. Yet you go about giving all the credit to the Divine Mother. You never say 'I'; you speak of God, Mother, She, Thou. If you are 'I am He,' why do you call God 'Thou?' "

The Master answered: "That is the ultimate matter of conduct. I have seen Him and embraced Him. I was infinite existence, Absolute Intelligence, and Bliss. But I could not stay in that unconditioned state and yet be here in the conditioned. There, there is no limit: each and all are one infinite existence, Unconditioned, Indescribable. You cannot use words about It. No matter what you say becomes finite. Naturally you say 'Thou, She, Mother.' Take the seven scales of music. Suppose you go on mounting—Do, re, mi—till you reach the highest note; what will you do next? You will come to Do. Each man after he has reached Silence, the highest pitch, the moment he opens his mouth he utters Do. And Do is God."

CHAPTER XI

A RECENT INITIATION

IN order to afford the reader some knowledge of the details, I shall describe the initiation of a friend of mine which took place recently. He and I had not met for the twelve years I was in America, and I had no knowledge that he had renounced the world and was doing certain spiritual exercises in order to attain Illumination. Hence I was quite surprised when I saw him one day in the robe of a Brahmachari, a novice, on the ferry-boat crossing from Calcutta to the Monastery. After the first pleasant shock of surprise at meeting him had passed, I looked at my friend's face. It was a sweet face in spite of his square jaw, narrow temples, pug nose and piercing eyes. It was in the corners of his mouth, notwithstanding his thin almost sharp lips, that sweetness dwelt. I felt as surprised at that discovery as the man who found in the nest of a Himalayan eagle, not that bird of prey but a dove.

By now the ferry-boat had reached the Monastery landing. We got off and walked towards the sacred grounds. There was no time to ask him many more questions. But I did ask one. His answer to it and many others he gave me on a morning about two months later.

It was about five in the morning—the day had just broken. He called me to go with him into a dilapidated garden. After meandering through abandoned groves of fruit trees and fragrant bushes, we reached a small enclosure where, under a banyan tree, lay a stone seat. My friend asked me to sit on it. Then he sat on the grass at my feet. The buzzing of insects and the rising heat of the day were all that one perceived in that spot. There was nothing else to distract us.

My friend shut his eyes for about a quarter of an hour and meditated. I sat there, watching his face. His complexion was olive, his forehead was high. He wore his hair, as all

Brahmacharis do, cropped most closely. His nose and ears were utterly plebeian. They were a little too thick, it seemed to me, but when I looked at his hands lying open on his lap, I was struck by their length and flower-like thinness. I noticed the strong and delicate lines in his palms sweeping up and across with a firmness as if they had been ploughed therein. The tips of his fingers rose like mounts of sensitiveness.

Hardly had I finished reading the lines in his hand when he opened his eyes and shot a glance at me. Now seeing me embarrassed he began: "It was when my father fell ill about eleven years ago that I came to the monastery to pray. I did not know why I was going there. You see, being the only son, and since my mother had died about half a year earlier, the entire care of my father had devolved upon me; it proved an extremely difficult task. But since circumstance rules life, I mustered all my courage and went to work. But every now and then a sense of fatigue used to seize me. It was under one of those spells of fatigue that I went to the Rama Krishna Monastery to pray.

"There, after I had prayed and performed the Arati (even-song), I felt renewed in strength, and went home. In a week I exhausted all the joy and strength I had garnered into my soul, so I returned to pray there once more. Again the same joy and strength came into my heart.

"It was about my third or fourth visit there that I stumbled upon Swami B——, my Guru. He happened to be a friend of my father's. Hence, finding me there, he asked about his health. Then, after I had told him how badly my father had been feeling, the Swami said to me, 'Come to see me when you feel like it.' You know how deep his voice was; it was also resonant like a vast gong. His words smote me like a command. Well, in a fortnight after that, my father grew better. He hoped to resume his work at the office soon. I hastened to the Monastery and told the good news to Swami. He listened with quiet attention. Then when my recital was over, he asked me: 'What are you going to do with yourself?'

" 'I do not know, my Lord. But my father wishes to see me married.'

" 'And you, do you wish it?'

"After weighing his words in my mind, I answered, 'No, I do not wish it.'

" 'Go, and meditate in the inner shrine; no one is likely to be there for the next two hours.'

"He dismissed me most summarily, I thought. But his command weighed on my mind. So I went into the shrine and meditated until dusk fell, when one of the monks came to prepare for Arati. I got up and left. On my way home on the ferry-boat I felt certain that I was going to become a monk.

"The next day while massaging my father, I said to him that I did not wish to marry because I wanted to be a holy man in order to attain Samadhi. I asked him to give me permission to renounce the world. He requested me to tell him my recent experiences. When I had done so my father said: 'You can go to the Swami to-morrow and tell him from me that you have my permission to renounce the world.'

"So I went to the monastery the next morning. But the Swami was not there. I went every day for a whole week, but found him not. At last on the tenth day I camped there from sunrise to sunset. It was about eight in the evening that he returned from the law courts where he had been giving evidence in a civil suit.

"He said to me as he seated himself on the platform of the Ghaut: 'I told the truth at the law courts but the lawyers believed me not. Like vultures they approach a dead body suspicious that it might be of a man feigning death. A beast becomes an expert of death yet suspects foul play from the dead. Lawyers are so used to extorting truth that when they hear it they dare not recognise it.'

"Then I told him what my father had desired me to say to the Swami. He sat quietly. In the light of the half-moon he appeared very calm and reserved. His voice had no resonance—it hardly rose above a whisper. He ended a short speech with this sentence.

'Very well, I will accept you as a Brahmachari next month. Think the matter over carefully in the meantime.' But just as I rose to go he remarked: 'Now that your father has given you freedom, what are you going to give him?'

" 'Give him, my Lord?' I asked.

" 'Yes. If he is free from selfishness, that ought to bring out unselfishness from you, since like begets like in this world.'

"I answered not a syllable—I had nothing to say. Quietly I took the dust from his feet and walked out into the dark. Two days before my taking the vow of a Brahmachari, I went into the inner shrine and meditated for a whole afternoon. (The truth suddenly came to me.) I went to the Swami and said: 'My Lord, I cannot be anything but a Brahmachari as long as my father lives, for I must serve him.'

"The Swami said: 'Good. I am glad to hear of your decision. I shall give you your first vow as I promised. After that you must study and meditate until you are ripe for the final initiation, which takes about ten years. These ten years instead of living with us here,

I give you permission to live with your father whom you love. And in the course of these years if you decide to marry, do so.'

"At the end of ten years I returned to the Swami and said, 'My Father is well again and urges me to renounce the world. He says that if I love him I should delay no longer. I will be initiated next week."

"What is this initial vow of a Brahmachari under which you have been living?" I asked my friend.

He answered, "I will tell you next week."

About five days later he was initiated. He now wore his ocher-colored robe, and the light that shone on his face was indescribable.

It was during one of those days that he told me the rest of his story in the same dilapidated garden. We stayed there a whole day talking to each other.

My friend said: "When the Swami gave me Brahmacharya I vowed to lead a life of celibacy, truthfulness and purity in thought, word and deed. Then he taught me three meditations which are difficult to describe. Let me see . . . suppose you conceive all life as purity—and exhale purity out of yourself, not only through every one of your brain cells but also between the beats of your heart and through the pores of your body. In the case of great yogis even the odor of their perspiration changes when they do it.

"The second meditation is similar. Suppose that you quicken your senses and emotions to feel that all life is Ahetuki Daya Sindhu—causeless currents of Love, that is, your life is a strong tide of Love uncaused by any motive. After about two or three years your heart becomes calm as a pool. Your mind grows clear like the eyes of a bird. All activities—even your breathing and eating—are characterised by a deep sanctity. Agitation and anxiety cannot come near you. Your breathing as well as your pulse never quickens, no matter what happens. Your deeds reiterate Love that has no cause.

"After the second stage, you begin to be sentient and possessed of great power. You can do your duties with perfect ease. You overcome all obstacles. You are sensitive to experiences which have been too subtle for you. You can read thoughts and hear silences.

"Now you are taught the last meditation: 'I renounce all power, even that of Love.' That was hard. It took me nearly five years. To renounce yourself is easy—but to renounce your unconscious thoughts and habits is difficult. Even your dreams must be purged of any sense of power and odor of miracles. Absolute surrender of your self to the One Self. You cannot do it alone. The teacher must pray and meditate with you—though you be at home over there and he in the monastery here. You gradually find out that not only he but others, strangers, are helping you. Who are they? They are the spiritual forces of life itself. As when you do evil, evil forces of life draw toward you, so, when you try to achieve selfless good, the good tendencies of life come to your aid. It is a supreme lesson in invisible co-operation. Thus through the help of others and by your own efforts you reach the threshold of Reality. Your holy man sends for you, for you are ripe for initiation at last. It is absolutely necessary to raise your concentration to the highest power. Your Master invites you to meditate with him, for he knows that you are ready. Many other holy men are invited to witness your last plunge. As all of them go on meditating on the same identical Truth, you gradually feel the presence of 'That' precipitated in your midst. As if the Lord, unable to resist such devotion, had come down to reward it by uncovering His Face. Just that instant your Guru touches the middle of your spine with his forefinger. That rends the veil. Lo! with these mortal eyes you see the Face of Immortality. The whole Universe is bathed in Light! Everything—from the dust of the road to the flight of a bird—throws away its vesture of appearance, and stands out like blades of bliss. Things are no more things, for they have become essences."

Here my friend stopped. He would speak no more. The silence that he had been alluding to seemed to rise between us. I waited for it to pass. After a long while when I felt that no sanctities were hovering about us, I asked my friend the question that seemed most important to me.

"Thank you," I said, "for what you have told me. But truly I do not want to know what you see or think. What I really want to know is how you feel."

"Feel?" asked my friend in bewilderment.

"Yes," I asked, "do you feel happy or unhappy? Do you feel one with the world, or apart from it? Are you hurt? Or——"

"I understand," he exclaimed with pleasure. "Though I feel happy I am acutely conscious of pain. I am aware of the pang that things and men inflict on one another. As an illustration of that let me describe to you Rama Krishna's experience. In the early days of his Illumination when he had not quite mastered its force he felt so one with the world that he bore marks of its pleasure and pain. One day, full of Oneness, he was standing on the river bank where a boat was moored. In a few minutes two of the boatmen started to quarrel. They struck each other. Rama Krishna, who was at least twenty yards away, yelled with pain. Then he ran in to the Kali temple and prayed to the Mother: 'Take away the sting of their quarrel from my body and soul. It hurts me so!' Hriday, his nephew, who had heard Rama Krishna's cry, hastened to find him. After looking about when he reached the temple, at last he found the Master crying and praying 'O Mother, remove the pain that is hurting the world. Free all of them from pain and hurt.' Then seeing Hriday he stopped praying and showed him the bruises on his own body. Hriday says that he cannot obliterate from his memory the terrible red stripes and black bruises on the Master's body. He also says that Rama Krishna was full of pain and bliss at the same time. Can you understand the contradictory nature of that state? If you can understand the Master's large experience, you will understand the petty one that is mine. How do I feel? I feel so blissful that all the pain of men and things that I see and perceive is mine. I am so close that I am identical with them. Yet I am apart. While I feel the pangs of their being, I go on feeling the bliss that is beyond their reach.

"Let me quote Shankara, who has a fine description of such an experience. 'As the clouds pass and repass in the sky, so do all the experiences fall within the soul in Oneness. And since all the black clouds cannot tarnish its emerald calm, so the pains and passions of the world cannot trouble the serenity of an illumined soul.'

"The pain of the world a holy man masters, and is not mastered by it. The difference between a holy man and a common soul in pain is that the former transcends it by his own power of vision and insight, while the latter has to have it removed from without."

Though my friend had told me his story very simply, yet after he had left me, it raised some questions in my mind that needed answering. Fortunately a day or two later I came across an old holy man who helped me over my difficulties. Let me picture it as it happened in life.

It was on a summer night. The sky was clear. The stars hung low. Behind them there was a haze almost tangible like a veil of silver, beyond it a shimmer of light like dust of gold which throbbed, then faded under the steep blue-black vault. The stars were so near and the Heavens so far! Below about us hung a jet black stillness which was broken by the occasional muttering noise of the palm fronds and the *Ka-la—Ka-la—Ka-la*—a cry of the Ganges flowing at our feet.

The man who sat next to me was old. I had seen his gray hair and hollow cheeks in daylight. I had also heard him expounding the Bhagabat in a classroom that afternoon. What he had said impressed me. It was because of that that I had brought him to the river bank. So I asked him my questions about Initiations in general and his own initiation in particular. I asked him: "What did it do to you?"

"Let us begin at the beginning," he remarked. "First of all you wanted to know about the final touch."

I said in agreement, "Yes, why does the Master help his disciple to experience Oneness? A man ought to win it by his own efforts."

After saying something to himself under

his breath, the old man began: "The purpose of a holy man's life is to find God, through his own efforts. But how can you find Him without getting some glimpse of Him ahead of time? Our form of initiation gives the initiate a brief look into the interior of his Spirit's Home. Once he has had that vision, no matter through whose assistance, he will always be homesick for it. And that nostalgia for another Vision of God will enable him to look above this world the rest of his life. He will not be tempted by the tawdry world of Time. That vision makes him safe from all except God, such is the power of it. That is why one has no right to take a disciple and train him if he cannot give his chela at least a temporary experience of Oneness with the Beloved."

"Can anyone," I questioned him further, "be given that experience by the touch of a real holy man?"

"Oh, no. There are souls that are ripe, and souls that are not." The holy man explained: "Even Rama Krishna himself could not give it to some souls. One time there came to him a fellow called Kaviraj—a sharp apothecary and doctor. He used to come and pray for training. But Rama Krishna maintained a certain coolness towards him. One day Kaviraj said: 'Why don't you give me your touch?' He repeated the question. At last brought to bay, Rama Krishna yielded. He gave the fellow the last touch—it is given by the holy man at a certain moment by bringing his forefinger in contact with the middle part of the novice's spine. No sooner had Rama Krishna touched him than Kaviraj howled and danced with pain. It was ghastly. The pain of the body is a picture of joy compared with the sight of a man literally screaming with pain in his soul. Rama Krishna then seized him in his arms and rubbed the poor fellow back to his normal state. Then he added: 'Not this life, my son. The touch of bliss has become cobra's venom in you. You are not ripe yet. Go on praying and meditating till you are. And when you have ripened yourself, if there is no one here, God Himself will come to earth to initiate you.' "

Now I asked the old holy man another

question: "But this final touch, is it not a sort of hypnotism?" Apparently he was not ready for it. In order to answer me, he waited and thought the matter over in his mind. At last, nearly a quarter of an hour later he, said:

"Hypnotism is quite different from the touch of a Master. Hypnotism is the impression of the will of one man upon another. Now in an initiation the disciple's will is not overcome but increased by his own meditations. He meditates and prays with eyes and ears shut. He breathes very slowly and rhythmically. His mind and heart are not kindled from outside. He goes inwards to his Self. Hour after hour he pierces his way into the heart of Silence. At last the teacher who has been sitting near him—with his eyes and ears shut—gives him the touch. That instant the initiate finds his own Self as the Mother of all the realities of the world. In other words, the whole process, both for the Master and the disciple, is not at all external. And the touch of the Master does not cause the disciple to lose his consciousness. On the contrary, the latter becomes all the more keenly conscious of joys and sufferings of men, women, beasts and plants around him. How different from a hypnotic state!

"When a man attains Illumination he becomes the will power, and the consciousness of all that are. His will, instead of becoming quiescent, becomes the will of the whole universe. His discrimination grows ever-sharp, his character ever-moral, his taste infallible, and his vision limitless."

After the holy man had stopped, the palm fronds muttered a little more loudly, making the air overhead full of eerie sounds while the Ganges, like a sharp knife, went on cutting the roots of the embankment on which we sat. An owl hooted and flew over us. I thought out my final question with care, then asked: "My Lord, now I understand what Illumination does to a man. But what is the difference between Illumination and Samadhi?"

The holy man cast a glance at the distant stars. Then at the twinkling lights of the city far to the south. He said: "The word Illumination is vague. You recall that there are three stages of spiritual realisation. First of all, a soul sees itself as the adorer of the Infinite. Through that adoration it finds fulfillment, claiming nothing for itself, and investing Him with all.

"Thou art the Path,
And the Goal that paths never reach;
Thou art the Lawful Lord
In Whom laws are lost
Like rivers in the sea.

"Thou feedest and sustainest
All that one sees, or seems;
Yet Thou art ever hungry for love,
And there is no end to Thy thirst for peace.

"Though all Time is as mail on Thy nakedness;
Though all space sandal thy feet,
Yet they are torn by the thorns of my prayers,
And Thy Body is pierced with bliss.

"All-healer, yet all wounds,
All-life, yet ever-dying,
All-praised, yet praiseless,
All-ending, yet no end for Thee!

"Thou art the agony of men,
Thou art the cry of the wounded beast,
Thou art the haughty mountain
And the eagle swooping down its side.

"The unborn that sings under its mother's
heart,
The battle-cry of the new-born child;
The song in the throat of the lover
And the pang of joy that brims in the eye of a
bride.

"Thou art the curve-pattern that bird-wings
make in the sky,
Thou art the trembling grass
And the tiger that creeps under it.

"Thou art the dark door of death,
Thou art the anguish of disease,
Thou the fear of the frightened,
And the secret shame of pride.

"In the reed the song,
In the string the tune,
Of the drum its beat.

"Thou art the taste in water,
Thou art the light in sun and moon,
The sounds fading into Silence,
And the sanctity of sacred Books.

"Thou art the diadem of Beauty,
Thou art the crown of Truth,
Thou art the scepter of Reality,
Thou art Good that destroys evil,
And Holiness that vanquishes Good.

"That," commented the holy man, "is the first stage of Illumination. The second level of the experience is attained when the devotee no more feels and adores God, but thinks himself a part of Him. With the exception of Rama Krishna, that is as far as the usual Guru's touch can take any disciple. This is the farthest reach of what is called Illumination. In that state you, as a part of God, are so highly conscious that all things live with you in God: you are aware of yourself as well as the selves of others with equal fulness. That is the farthest that Illumination can take you. But when you attain Samadhi, you go beyond. Words cannot describe how far beyond you go. You recall that line in the Upanishads—

"'*Aham asmi prathamaja ritasya*—I am more ancient than the effulgent Gods. For I am the first-born of the Essences. I am the artery of Immortality, Amritsya Nabhai!' That is what happens to one when he attains Samadhi: he becomes that artery of Immortality which feeds and sustains all the other realities of experience. Though in that state your heart stops beating, and your mind seems extinguished, yet you are more alive and more conscious than ever before. Because you have become the sap of Truth that nourishes All."

"Could Rama Krishna—could he not—give you an experience of Samadhi?" I asked.

He answered: "He is the only Master that could. Not any other holy man had the same abundance of spirituality as he. Others gave you Illumination. But his touch lifted you on the highest plane of Samadhi. Now you understand, my son," concluded the holy man, "that illumination is unity with all the realities, while Samadhi is your identity with the *One* Reality in all."

He looked all round, at the river, the far-off city, and the heavens above. "The night has advanced far. It is time for sleep. Farewell, my son." He rose to go. "Samadhi should be experienced. It can't be explained." Now he lifted his face to the stars and chanted: "O Night, thou mirror of Silence . . ." Then turning to me he whispered: "Samadhi is your realisation of that Oneness that turns your Self into the Matrix of the Universe: *'Nityo nityanam . . .*

"The Eternal behind all eternal,
The consciousness that crouches behind all consciousnesses,
The One that is caught, then slips out of the Many,
The taller than the tallest,
The minuter than the minutest,
That cry of Silence
In the clamor of realities.
The Truth of all truths,
And the Godhood of God."

CHAPTER XII

HOLY MAN OR INCARNATION OF GOD

THE best testimony that I have read of Rama Krishna's holiness is from the pen of the late Swami Premananda. He died before I reached the Monastery, so the only way in which I could touch the hem of his garment was through his writings. But I must say a word about the man even at second-hand before I translate his epistles.

He was a very haughty Brahmin before he met his Master. Though not so stately as Vivekananda and Turyananda, yet he was a man of great charm. His Roman nose, strong mouth, and square chin betokened a man of action and decision. But that side of his features was fully balanced by his spacious brow and compassionate eyes. "Whenever he looked at people he poured love into them," say those who knew him.

In his early youth, Premananda developed great independence of character. While he was studying at the University in spite of all the advice of his parents and the ridicule of his friends, he paid frequent visits to the Holy One of Dakshineswar. The very first time the Master saw him he was questioned: "My boy, have you thought out where you belong?" He made no answer for the time being.

Five months later one afternoon Premananda brought his parents with him and said to the Master: "I know where I belong, I have brought my parents so that they can see with their own eyes what kind of a holy man I wish to serve." From that day he was given his lessons in meditation until about six years later when he was initiated. After he had attained Soul-illumination his new name was revealed. He abandoned the homely name, Baburam, that his parents had given him. From now on he was called Premananda—Bliss of Love.

His love, though all embracing, he showed in its fulness to the younger generation in whom he took the most painstaking interest. Not only did he help them to solve their spiritual problems, but he also aided them in their athletic activities. If the young boys needed a football field they went to him, and he always secured one for them; if they needed boats to row on the Ganges it was he who commandeered them from the monastery. Because of this, every young man of our generation who knew Premananda loved him. Though he was past fifty, and my contemporaries were only lads of sixteen or seventeen, yet his relation to them was that of a captain to his football team.

I did not know him personally but what I had heard of him all those years had endeared him to me. So it was natural that I should be deeply elated when I came upon Premananda's written testimony about Rama Krishna. I hastened to translate it. It is necessary to warn the reader that Premananda was no luke-warm believer. He believed Rama Krishna to be an Incarnation of God. He placed him on the same level with Jesus and Buddha. Yet he was fully aware of the difference between his Master and the other two. For he says: "The present Incarnation of God radiates renunciation in every shape and form. Each one of God's Incarnations has its peculiarity. Think of feeding five thousand souls to repletion with five loaves of bread, walking on water, ascending to Heaven, making trees bear fruit to feed multitudes.

"But such strange characteristics I fail to see in the new Incarnation: Rama Krishna does no miracle.

"Then behold this: almost all previous Incarnations shed a glow of beauty that filled the world. But Rama Krishna lacks even that. When Girish asked the Master, 'Why no glory of Form this time?' The Blessed One answered, 'In my days of prayer and penance I prayed:

"I want no physical beauty or glory, O Mother,
Give me only Illumination of the Soul!

"He lacked beauty of form; also beauty of mind, for he was no scholar. Other Incarnations before him confounded the learned men of their time at a very early age. Buddha exhausted all the learning of his time only to despair of salvation, and that he milked the udders of the Upanishads there is no doubt. Lo! our Incarnation—by straining all his intellect and gasping with the last breath of his mind—all he could do was to read and write a little. Yet scholars used to crawl away from him to hide their scholarship. His effect on them was that of the sun on owls. Why did they crawl away like earthworms into the darkness of the earth? Because he came from where their discussions could not reach. You cannot conceive all of the holy city, Benares, by looking at its map. Only he who is the citizen of the eternal—Benares the Timeless—knows it. Rama Krishna knew how to unlock every door of the Timeless for he held the key of Immortality in his hands.

"Rama Krishna had another peculiarity. Other Incarnations preached their respective beliefs. But he never preached a belief. One night long past the middle of it, I heard him walk up and down the verandah spitting. I went out to find what was happening to him. He was spitting, and praying thus: 'O Mother, do not bring me honor by bringing me creed-believers. Propound no creed through me.' Then he said to me: 'Don't run after name and fame. Go across the dirty waters of all fame and all names—reach the shore of the Nameless. Let people come to get what they want from you; then they must go away. Be like a flower—blossom to your fulness. Let the bees rifle your heart. May the world be enchanted; but hold none captive by the beauty of your Soul.'

"Other Incarnations have insisted on their own light, and there have been some who held theirs to be the only light. But our Lord says: 'As many lights as there are devoted pilgrims! If He is infinite, the roads to Him must be infinite also.' Rama Krishna lived so that he elicited the inner truth of every religion. And we are here not to quarrel about our differences, but to find God. If we lose Him, we shall sink in a sea of torture, sin, and pain. Therefore find Him by all means. Why bother about roads?

"Enter the garden, eat its sweet mangoes, and depart. You did not enter the garden to count the leaves on the mango tree. Why waste time discussing whether worship of God should be through idols or without idols? Is He with form or without it? It does not matter whether the theory of Reincarnation is all sound.

"If you want to know of the Eternal City, then ask those who have been to Benares. Having heard all they have to say go forth, enter, and be its citizen. But if you stay at home and discourse: 'The sacred City is thus. Oh! no, it is not thus,' you may go on that way for a thousand times, yet it will bring you not even a hair's breadth nearer Benares. Whether I was born here before or not has no relation to the resolve that I will see Him here and now in this life. Rigid belief in a creed is not helpful, but may do harm to your soul. If you know Him you won't be bothered by religious doctrines! You may read and believe all the scriptures and revealed words of all the Sons of God, yet you will not be able to find God. You must rise above books and

Teachers; and behold Him whom they beheld. Then all the mysteries will suddenly unlock their secrets to you!

"He, your Self, has the Key. Beg for His Compassion. Consecrate your life to Him. God is not to be trapped by the regimentation of rituals. He wants to be caught by your heart, by your longing, by your sincerity.

"However, along with his peculiarity each Incarnation embodied for the world a certain ideal. Not that He lacked other ideals. But it was always one of them that dominated the rest. Buddha embodied the ideal of living without earthly desires and dreams. He was unattached through and through. He was so unattached that he did not even want salvation for himself. He wanted others to have it.

"After Buddha came Shankara, the ideal of wisdom. When a mere stripling he was asked by his teacher: 'Whence do you come; who are you; wither bound?' Shankara answered:

"I am not in the senses, nor in the mind.
I am not in touch, nor am I taste;
Breathing and beating of the heart
Even they can hold me not;

Eyes that see, see me not;
Ears that hear, hear not my silence!
For I am not the earth, nor in the air;
The light that scorches, and the spaces of
ether,
Even they are tongue-tied when they seek to
name me;
For I am infinite knowledge,
I am Life that is behind the living,
I am the Absolute,
Existence infinite . . .
I am Bliss.

"Shankara embodied wisdom. And to fulfil that wisdom later came the Incarnation of Love—Chaitanya. They, all the Incarnations, imply each other. While the rabble think, they quarrel. To end all such quarreling came Rama Krishna. He has verified all the religions by his living, and bound them together by their common aim: realisation of God. It is because he was so full of love and compassion that Rama Krishna became the embodiment of Tolerance and Insight. An example of his compassion is found when he made a pilgrimage to Benares. Seeing the poor and the destitute, he said to the rich man who took him there: 'I will not go hence to see the holy of holies until these are fed and clothed.' Again, when he was dying of cancer of the throat, one day no one came to ask him for food, shelter, or spiritual light. It made him forget his pain: he wailed, 'How I suffer because none have needed my help to-day.'

"He, who had to give up speaking and eating, yet cried aloud for others! Such was his compassion. I have seen, watched and nursed him a year and a half. Each and every day he thought of someone to help.

"He was never idle—always at work, gardening, sweeping the rooms; petty little miscellaneous work of the Monastery he did without losing the purpose of his life. He disliked disorder. Even filling a Pan-leaf with nuts and Chunam—mere woman's work this—he taught me how best to do it. He was so practical.

"He did not accept any religious teaching on any hearsay. He proved its merits through practice. And that is why all religions led him to the same God.

"Not only through all religions, but in all

beings he saw the Lord. He had no preferences. He was intoxicated with the love of all creatures. He never succumbed to forming groups and denominations. He who sees God in all, and all things in God, needs no creed to fence himself in. The jewel of spirituality needs no casket. And the day we, the sons of Rama Krishna, go in for doctrines and creed-mongering will be our last hour before darkness and downfall. A river needs no fences. Only ponds are fenced in. No wonder they become poisoned in time. He has warned us against such sinister evils as calling ourselves 'We are Rama Krishnites'—'No soul can be saved without Rama Krishna,' 'Therefore all must embrace Rama Krishnaism.' Beware of such quarrels! Beware!

"Our scriptures say that holiness gives one power over one's entire self. Had you seen him you would have believed it. He had perfect dominion over each vein, each cell, and every blood corpuscle of his body. Though his throat pained him excruciatingly, yet when we wanted to wash it with medicine and were afraid to inflict further pain on him, he would say, 'Wait . . . now wash.' Then he would remove his consciousness from that spot. Though we would do all that medical science ordered, yet he would feel no pain. It is because he controlled all of his body, heart, mind, and soul. Like all full-grown Yogis, he could suspend the action of his heart and yet live. He could withdraw consciousness from any part of his self. I am not telling stories. I have witnessed with mine own eyes what I am setting down here.

"Yet he lived in his body. How could he do it? He answered me once: 'A fully realised soul, no matter who, lives as little in the body as does the meat inside a dried up fruit —just clinging slightly to one side of the skin.'

"He had no caste and said: 'Devotees of God are beyond any caste.' Sometimes I have seen him unable to eat food offered by the high and mighty, because the food was not offered by a pure heart. But sometimes he would eat from the plate of an outcast. One such outcast said: 'Don't, Sir, don't—I have eaten forbidden food.' But Rama Krishna went on eating and said: 'Your food is pure because your heart is sinless.' If anybody offered him anything wishing for a boon, he never accepted it. Yet at the same time he could not abide those who were puritans, suffering from a perpetual fear of contamination. 'Too much concentration on purity becomes a plague. People stricken with that fell disease find it hard to think of God.'

"One of our fellow disciples felt himself too weak to follow the spiritual path. He came to Rama Krishna and unburdened his heart's secret. The Master said: 'Very well, Vakil-at-nama (give me the power of attorney to represent you before God).' Now this is the severest thing to do, for it demands the strictest sincerity on the part of the giver. If he is sincere through and through, then his Master can work for him. For the man who has such sincerity has so much power that he can command anything. That is what really happens. Rama Krishna said: 'To give your Master the task of realising God for you is to renounce yourself so that you grow totally indifferent to the material world of good and evil!'

"About books on philosophy and religion—

he had a book with him entitled 'Salvation—Its Realisation.' We used to read it to him. He explained his love of books thus. 'As long as you read about Him you are in His mood. You cannot meditate all the time, so fall back on the second best thing—reading about Him. Since the zephyr does not blow from the sea to cool you, you had better fan yourself with a fan.'

"About places of pilgrimage, he held that 'He who has no God within will not find Him in a holy city. He who has the Lord in his heart will find Him there. Men bring sanctity with them to a place and make it holy. It is men's purity that makes a place of pilgrimage, otherwise how can a place purify a man?'

"So with the blessings of Rama Krishna, sink yourselves in spirituality and do not stop sinking till you find the bottom—Him. God is not to be found by discussion, but through realisation. We must realise Him in our present life and by every possible means. Without Him there is no pathway to bliss. And nothing on earth can give you Peace without Him."

Premananda's paper ends here. He has perfect faith that Rama Krishna was an incarnation of God. But what about those who do not share that faith? Rama Krishna himself answers: "All pathways lead to the same God." And one of the laws the Monastery lays down is this: "He who believes Rama Krishna to be a mere holy man is just as right as he who calls him an Incarnation of God." And if I were to give any advice to the reader, I should say, "It does not matter what anybody says; what really matters is the life that Rama Krishna lived. If the example of that life does not quicken our spirituality then no amount of words about him and from him can make any difference."

CHAPTER XIII

RAMA KRISHNA AND A WAYWARD SOUL

OF Rama Krishna's many disciples Girish Ghose, the playwright, proved to be the most difficult. He was recognised as a man of genius before he was thirty. It was about that age that he lost his wife, and with her his faith in God. "How can God exist if He lets perish those who are young and beautiful?" He did not rest with such a question. He studied all the religions of the world for an answer to it. But they failed to satisfy him. Of course in the meantime his companionship with the Bohemians of Calcutta theaters went on undermining his moral powers. It was about five years after his wife's death, that finding no solace in religion, Ghose flung himself into unlimited dissipation. In a short time he became known as a drunkard. What looked strange to most people is that under the influence of liquor he wrote two religious plays that ran for five years. Though he found little in any faith to sustain him, yet he found in the life of religious teachers abundant inspiration for his plays such as *Buddha, Chaitanya, and the Medieval Saint Billwamangal* (based on the life of Tulsidas). The last named play has been adapted into English and published under the title "Chintamani—the quest of the Infinite."

In all those plays Girish had a thesis to maintain, namely: "Religions are dreary and hard, but religious men are inspiring and compassionate." It was his study of the lives of the saints that made him all the more curious to find one in real life. Girish, whenever he was sober, searched for a holy man that measured up to his expectations. Though most of the holy men he met disappointed him, yet he kept an open mind in the matter.

At last one of his friends brought him the news that there was a holy man living at Dakshineswar who would satisfy his curiosity. There is a legend that Girish got gloriously drunk before he set out to meet Rama

Krishna. No doubt he did that in order to annoy the man of God whom at their first meeting he insulted again and again. He said repeatedly: "I don't care for God, and what's more, though drinking is a sin, I drink just to show what I think of your God." Rama Krishna answered: "But drink to God. Maybe He too drinks." Girish demanded angrily: "How do you know?" Rama Krishna answered: "If He did not drink, how could He have created this topsy-turvy world?" That took all the wind out of the sails of Girish.

Then he asked: "What is a Guru?" Rama Krishna answered: "A Guru is a man who introduces another man to God. What's more, you have a Guru of your own if you would consent to recognize him." This particular hint was utterly lost on the inebriated Girish.

Yet in order to give time for the thought to sink into the mind of Girish, Rama Krishna changed the subject by requesting: "Let me visit your theater, please."

Girish answered: "Very well, you are welcome any day you choose." After Girish had taken his departure, some critical soul said to the Master: "What a vile fellow! What do you find in him?"

"A great devotee of God," was the Blessed One's cryptic answer.

In a few days Rama Krishna went to see Girish act in one of his plays. At the end of the play Girish took all the curtain calls, for he was a vain man. Later on, when the Holy One came to the green room to offer him his modicum of praise, Girish, full of audacity, asked him in a voice of studied modesty: "I am so glad that my acting has pleased you. Can you tell me what it lacks?"

Rama Krishna, without the slightest haste or hesitation, gave this opinion: "You are suffering from crookedness of Soul."

Girish questioned eagerly: "How can I lose it, my Lord?"

The Master advised: "You need Religion badly."

Those words annoyed Girish. He who had never taken anyone's advice before was so enraged by Rama Krishna that he lost his temper, and forthwith called the Master all the names with which his drunkard's mind was fertile. In a few moments it became quite apparent that the Blessed One had expected something of the sort, for there he stood, calm as a log, listening to Girish. When the latter had finished he spoke a word of blessing, then left for Dakshineswar. Of course the very next morning Girish sent one of his intimate friends to Rama Krishna to pray for forgiveness on his behalf. That emissary of his knew the Teacher too well to plead for forgiveness. Instead he said: "Girish is too great a man to perish of drink, my Lord."

The Master answered: "But he uses such hard words."

"You must bear them," answered the friend.

That made the Master smile. He asked with a twinkle of mischief in his eye: "Suppose he beats me to death?"

The friend answered: "That too you will bear, my Lord. He can't give you what he has not got. He gives abuse and violence as a snake gives out venom."

On hearing Girish's friend speak thus, Rama Krishna requested: "Get me a carriage at once, please, I must go and see him! Can you take me to his home?"

When he reached the house, he found Girish very tipsy. But Rama Krishna spoke to him with as much regard for his judgment as if he were talking to a sober man. That produced the desired effect on Girish. Instead of losing his temper—he listened to the Holy One's speech. The latter stayed with him till he fell sound asleep.

From that day on he became attached to Rama Krishna. But just the same he could not give up drinking, nor could he eschew the company of his Bohemian friends.

The tactics that Rama Krishna used on him are worth recording. One day Girish came to Dakshineswar in his carriage. He was quite sober. Seeing him coming through the garden, Rama Krishna said to one of his chelas: "I see he is sober, but there is a flask of liquor in his carriage. You fetch it to me in secret." Girish came and seated himself in the Master's presence, who was discoursing on the Lord. The hours passed rapidly, and with their passage Girish grew thirstier and thirstier. At last, unable to bear it any longer, he rose to go to his carriage. But Rama Krishna stopped him: "You do not have to fetch it. I had it fetched. Here is the flask. Drink, my son."

From that day on, Girish drank less and less. And years later when he drank no more, he is reported to have said: "You know why I gave up drinking. It is because my Guru, Rama Krishna, never commanded me to. He not only gave us holiness, but also freedom. He asked us to do nothing for his sake."

But Girish's problem was more than drunkenness. His real difficulty lay in his horror of austerity. He longed to realise the Lord, yet he would not pray, nor meditate. People knew that he was impatient, and too fond of pleasure to perform any of the difficult rites prescribed in the scriptures.

As his intimacy with Rama Krishna increased, instead of finding peace of mind he felt more and more troubled. Once he asked: "Suppose I give up the company of my Bohemian friends. Shall I do it for the sake of my religion?"

"No. That is not necessary. You must not give up the fallen," advised the Master. "God comes to earth for them. Are you purer than God?"

The very next time he came to see the Master he asked: "Shall I give up drinking? Would not that bring me nearer God?"

"Your giving up anything will not get you far if you do not meditate and pray. You drink less and less every day; has that brought you nearer the Lord? You cannot hoodwink the Absolute by such theatrical acts."

"What am I to do? I can't pray. I can't meditate."

Rama Krishna suggested no other remedy that day. So Girish took his leave. The following fortnight he made every effort to pray and meditate on the Beloved. Alas! it did not succeed. At last he felt desperate. "This business of prayers must be settled one way or another." Saying so, he dressed himself in the height of style, as was his wont, and set out for Dakshineswar; for he wanted speech with his Guru.

He found the latter in his room, surrounded by some disciples. Rama Krishna, who was talking to them, interrupted himself and spoke to Girish directly. It did not take him long to learn of Girish's trouble. He also gathered from the wretched fellow's lips that he had become desperate; he said that he preferred suicide to prayers and meditation.

"But, Girish, I am not asking you to do too much. Just think of the Lord a moment before eating your meals, and once before going to sleep. I think if you sincerely carry out those rites, that will be enough. Can you not do that?"

After a long pause, Girish answered with fearful finality: "I cannot do that, my Lord. I am an artist. I do not know when I eat, nor where I sleep." He pondered again awhile. After carefully weighing every word he said: "I hate routine. I cannot stand hard and fast rules. I won't pray; I won't meditate. I cannot think of God even for one moment."

Those words made Rama Krishna think awhile. Then he said: "If you want to see the Lord, and since you will not take a single step forward to meet Him, there is only one choice left. Can you give me Vakil-at-nama (power of attorney)?"

"Power of Attorney? What do you mean, my Lord?" questioned the bewildered Girish.

Rama Krishna explained: "I mean give me the right to pray for you. Do you want me to pray for you? From now on be a true artist, eating what is given, sleeping where you can, asking nothing of anybody. You have no responsibility of any kind. Accept everything that happens, and ask for nothing for yourself. You must live by this rule: TVAYA HRISHIKESHA HRIDISTHITENA, YATHA NIYUKTOSMI TATHA KAROMI—AS THOU WILLEST FROM WITHIN ME, O SUBTLE MASTER, SO SHALL I DO. Promise to live absolutely at the mercy of the Lord."

Girish agreed and gave his Guru the Power of Attorney then and there. He resolved to live, "like a leaf, at the mercy of the sun and the wind; or, like a kitten, utterly dependent on the mother-cat who might bring her charge up in a royal bed or in a garbage can. Complete resignation!"

Rama Krishna was a hard taskmaster. He now began to train Girish in his new attitude. It was difficult for the latter to demand nothing of anybody. Day after day this Bohemian had to go without what he wanted until it was given to him. But he stuck to his promise to Rama Krishna. One day in his company the Master heard Girish say, "I will do this."

"What did you say, Girish?" questioned Rama Krishna. "You have no will to do the slightest act of selfishness. You are not to do anything, for I have the Power of Attorney. Remember, you live and move as the Lord within you wills. I am praying for you, but all my prayers will be set at naught if you do not renounce all initiative."

From that time on, a great change began to work in Girish. He saw that to surrender one's responsibility to another is to surrender one's self to the Self of the Universe, which forces one to live without any desire for personal happiness. But, headstrong as ever, he stuck to his promise, and by doing so he grew very religious. And in a short time he became one of the important spiritual forces of his time. He toiled at his art all the harder. No doubt because of that he became our greatest modern dramatist—in fact there is none between him and Kalidasa, Bhababhuti, and Vasa of the classical age.

Not only was he our greatest modern playwright; he was also a great actor and producer. It was he who revealed to the women of the underworld that they could change their lives for the better by taking up acting as a trade. Many wretched souls he saved by training them to act. Not only that, he also lifted up and revealed to the eyes of the public at least half a dozen actresses of the highest rank, who had been hitherto condemned to a life of vice while boys played the parts of women on the stage. Since Girish, all that has been changed.

The other day in India when one of his star actresses, now an old woman, called on my wife and myself, she told us how "Father"—that is what she called Girish—worked. "He brought about a revolution in the life of womanhood in general. Women in terrible penury, instead of being forced down into the abyss of vice, were now rescued by the stage. But 'Father' did not stop there. He brought us all in touch with the teachings of Rama Krishna. He wanted us to come to the Monastery during the hours of worship and pray to God. Some of us were afraid lest we soil the sacred grounds. Father answered: 'If Rama Krishna were living he would teach you and me himself. He loves us. Didn't he come to earth for the fallen like ourselves?' "

Our talks with many other old actors and actresses convinced us that Girish, by staying with his old Bohemian companions, did more spiritual good than if he had left them. After his soul's second birth, he did not act like a moral parvenu; he repudiated nothing of his past. Instead, he slowly permeated his friends and his writings with the spirit of Rama Krishna. And as for the Power of Attorney that he gave his Guru, Turyananda and others testify that he never violated it. All of them affirm, "Girish was the most religious of us all: he lived, as he said he would, by the promptings of the Indweller." Even at death's door he did not forget the Power of Attorney, for with his last breath he prayed: "This madness of matter is a terrible veil—remove it from mine eyes, O Rama Krishna!"

CHAPTER XIV

MAHAPRASTHAN OR LAST JOURNEY

I HAVE already alluded to the fact that towards 1885 it became quite clear that Rama Krishna was stricken with cancer of the throat. The Master reiterated to his disciples that the time was fast approaching when he would not be in their midst. No doubt that intimation saddened them all, and in order to rise equal to the occasion, all of them intensified their spiritual practices considerably. Vivekananda, the leading spirit of the band, urged them thus: "The Master is seriously ill. Who knows how long he will remain in the body? Let us strive hard to serve him by more prayers and meditation. If we do not work hard now, we shall repent after he is gone. Let us not waste our time in working out our petty human plans. Let not desire and worldliness fasten their tentacles upon us. Let us toil till we live divinity, breathe divinity, and act the will of God."

As soon as it was established that the Master was incurably sick, people began to come to him, and urged him to cure himself miraculously. Each one of them said: "Master, if you are a saint, you can heal yourself."

Rama Krishna, whose throat hurt him every time he spoke, said to them: "Why make such silly proposals? This, here"—meaning himself—"was given up to God once and for all. How can I, or anyone, stoop to withdraw it?"

During this period of sickness, Rama Krishna concentrated almost all his attention on his own disciples. "This disease marks out the inner group from the outer. Those who have renounced all, live here. They belong to the inner mansion. They must strive together and create the Being which will inspire men and women for centuries to come."

Though the disease progressed rapidly during the ensuing year, yet he spared himself no pains: he instructed his band of chelas. He poured into their mind and soul all that he had within himself. Since no solid food could pass through his throat, he drank a little milk now and then. But milk could not sustain that tall frame of his, and the more his strength failed the more he imposed hard spiritual practices on his disciples.

That was particularly so in the case of Vivekananda and the "holy mother," for on them rested the leadership of the rest. The Master said to them: "I leave them in your care."

Within a year and a half the terrible disease wrought ghastly ravages in the Master's body. At last the end was in sight. Even then people came to urge him to do the miracle of curing himself. Not only outsiders, but also one or two of his disciples urged him to do so. But he answered them: "I cannot cure myself for I have no will of my own. It is God's Will now."

Every day it grew more and more difficult to make him lie in bed. He wished to sit up and speak to them—to unburden himself of all that he had realised. He sat in bed, propped up with pillows, and discoursed to each disciple on the problems that were before him.

On an afternoon in July it became quite evident that the end would come soon. The Master was in great pain, yet he insisted on sitting up in bed. He had his way. His beard had grown longer. The corners of his mouth were drawn in pain, but his dark, long slanting eyes blazed with light. That light, like the tide of a river, rose high and higher, then flooded his entire face. It was so beautiful and so powerful that no one could look at it long. The disciples had to look away until the Master withdrew the light. Sometimes he would stay thus for forty-five minutes. Then he would speak; though it hurt him like the sting of a hundred cobras, yet he answered the questions that rose in their minds. He did not wish to die without telling his disciples the last thing they wanted to know. With a firmness not of this world he said:

"Why am I explaining all I know to you? Because I brought you with me. No Teacher comes to earth without his own band of faithfuls. It is they who understand him first. Then they explain him to the world. I am telling you all, so that you will be able to explain without any obscurity and without any magic the simplicity of Truth. . . . You and I came to earth as a band of minstrels. Minstrels sing at the door of every house, then depart—no one cares to know their name. We have sung at the doors of the earth! When we depart they will not know our hidden names. . . . Pain is unavoidable so long as the spirit must speak through forms. It is the body—the form—that suffers. . . . One must renounce matter. If a man sits on a cushion and you want it, you must move him in order to find it. So must one remove materialism to find spirituality beneath. In course of time, every one of you will find the Spirit saturating all. But that comes later. . . ." Here he pointed at a disciple and remarked: "He moves about like a naked sword, while the one yonder—Hirananda—is docile, but full of the sting of the Spirit;

like a cobra under the charmer's flute—quite docile but the power to sting is there." He was silent for a while then he said quietly, as if making his own mind clear on the point: "To-day I gave you all. I am taking nothing with me. I am a beggar now. Depend no more on me, nor on any other man. Depend on Him. It is through His power that you will act. Through His power you will do great kindness to the world. After that is done, you, the Minstrels, will return to the House of Song whence you came."

Just then the dusk fell. Suddenly he passed into Samadhi. His breathing ceased; his heart beat no more, and his pulse stopped. His body became stiff. By the light of the lamps the apostles watched him. At midnight he came out of Samadhi and spoke for nearly an hour. About one in the morning he entered into Samadhi again. His hair stood on end. His eyes, half-closed, brimmed with light. A smile that rose on his lips deepened and spread over his entire face. Then it began to ebb slowly from his brow and cheeks. It passed back to the corners of his mouth.

There it flickered like a flame for several moments, then suddenly his lips hardened, and with it that ebbing smile froze into the rigidity of death.

CHAPTER XV

TURYANANDA'S CONCLUSION

I HAVE intimated in a previous chapter that I intended to deal at length with Swami Turyananda's work. He was one of the disciples of Rama Krishna whom I knew. And since he is not living now, I think I may speak about him without any reserve.

I have already alluded to his great power and prestige among other holy men. At his feet I learnt more about the heart of the religious teachings of India than I can set forth in writing. It was because of his Himalayan spiritual stature that I returned to him to obtain a final measurement of the Message of Rama Krishna.

Now the Monastery in Benares, over which Turyananda presided, was divided into two sections, separated from each other by a high concrete wall. One of them was called Gunatita and the other Saguna.

In the former lived about a dozen monks who through meditation and concentration sought to realize the Gunatita—God without any name or form. They held no rites and rituals. Their days were spent in learning concentration and acquiring Insight. They were the most devoted of scholars as well. They studied all the Indian systems of philosophy and those of the West. Their dwelling, a two-storeyed brick building, gave one the impression of unmitigated somberness. Every wall, every door and every stick of furniture had no useless decoration. Beauty had been reduced to bare essentials in this home of Silence and Meditation. I do not know why Turyananda, who was a Yogi and holy man, never lived in the Gunatita section.

On the contrary, he dwelt in the Saguna part of the Monastery. Saguna (Through name and form) worship consists in realising God through work, prayer, rituals, observances and festivals. In fact the word Saguna covered a multitude of practices, such as feeding the hungry, succoring the needy, ministering to the sick and giving instruction to those who asked for it. Owing to the range of the activities that the Saguna worshippers undertook, they had to own an estate full of buildings of all kinds, and large gardens. In a remote corner of the latter, under some tall trees, stood the hut of Turyananda. Since I have dwelt in another place elaborately with Turyananda's conception of salvation by good works, I shall not go into the matter here. Let us learn from his lips the import of the message of Rama Krishna.

It was on a morning in June that I presented myself at the door of Turyananda's hut. After entering, I found its interior filled as usual with cool shadows. There was not much sunlight within, but the atmosphere was clear enough to afford me a distinct vision of every person and object in the room. Turyananda, clad in the ocher robe of Sanyasins, sat on a couch in the middle of the room. One glance at his face made it more than vivid to me that he was all-holy. I took the dust from his feet, then crouched on the floor before him. Now I looked at him very carefully. This time that lion-like person was pouring upon me a sweetness and tenderness that were indescribable: his eyes, his mouth, even the slight forward inclination of his head, all showered on me the benediction of a lover and a seer. He gazed on me I know not how long, when those smiling lips opened and in a deep voice (deep as a bull-frog's, we say) he said: "You have certain questions for my ear, my son." "Yes, my Lord, it is about your Master, and about this Monastery."

"About Him, all of you know my feeling. May He bless you with illumination."

"My Lord," I began again, "if I understand Rama Krishna's stature at all, it is because I have beheld you."

"You mean, a dwarf like me conveys to you the Himalaya-humbling height of his soul?" Then Turyananda laughed out loud. It was a very simple laugh; not a trace of malice in it, but plenty of mischief. He laughed so that tears stood in his eyes. It took him a little time to wipe his eyes dry with an end of his robe. "Please repeat your question to me."

I said: "Please don't laugh at it. I want

to know many things. But the question that I should like to ask first is about your work. Why do you live here in the Saguna section? Is Saguna worship really better than the Gunatita?"

Never in a hurry, Turyananda pondered a little. He put his hands together—then looked at them. Now fixing his gaze on me he began: "In the Gunatita—beyond name and form—the monks practise the arts of concentration, and study Vedanta texts along with other metaphysics. They are in a hurry to find Him, so they think of Him all the time. When they cannot practise concentration they read the sacred books. Thus they keep themselves—mind and body—consecrated to one subject. The only times they interrupt their work are when they eat their solitary meal and sleep. They do not sleep much either. It is a hard life. But that is the price you pay for giving up the simpler path of name and form."

"But, my Lord, you are one of the great holy men of our time. Why don't you go to the other side? Why do you stay and work here in this world?" I asked with impatience.

He laughed again. This time it was a gentle laughter. After the zephyr of mirth had subsided, he resumed: "It is well that I accept every epithet that comes my way. For a man who is a votary of God must accept whatever is hurled at him—a cow-dung cake or a lotus-flower. As to why I do not go over to the other side, my son, your answer is in Rama Krishna. If He who became God stayed on this side, after his realization, why not the smaller fry like myself? Then they who are working in and through Saguna name and form, are as sacred as those on the other, Gunatita, side. These here are probably more sacred for they are more numerous. God comes to earth for them. Then there is more fun to be had here. Think of the kind of questions like yours that are asked to quicken our vanity. And after all, as our Master says, that to earn salvation for one's own self is not amusing enough—I really mean amusement, since God is the Most Absorbing Amusement. You must see the light in order to give sight to the blind, which is most amusing. The more numerous the ways of reaching Him, all the more formidable grows the consensus of opinion that He exists. If you love God, and if you have seen Him your way, it is to your own interest to urge others to see Him through their unique methods. How else can you know that your way (of religion) has given you the ultimate God, if all the other religions do not reveal Him every time a soul plunders the secret of Immortality? Rama Krishna taught us the ancient truth of India —ATMANO MOKSHARTHA JAGAT JANA HITAYACHA (the blessings that will come to all and the salvation that will be yours). Where else but in this part can one pursue both? One like myself likes this Saguna worship. Each name and each form that is, exists in order to articulate God. We must help all people to utter the thunder of Silence. Let the gem of salvation be set in the heart of every man and woman. For each one of them is here to give you verification of your God by finding Him in his way."

"That explains why you who can easily cross over any time to the Gunatita, Absolute, stay here on this side of name and form?" I asked.

"I stay on this side," he said emphatically,

"because it is the easier of the two. It is the path of the weak and the simple. Here is room for a man of action, for a pure mystic, and for a pure lover of God. The man of action, if he eschews all the material reward of his acts here or hereafter, will find God in no time. A mystic who meditates and prays without any desire for acquiring power, he too will find the All-Powerful in a short time. And he, who loves God's creatures, finds Him the instant his love is not caused by a motive, nor held by an earthly end. Here in the house of name and form there is room for all. It is the market place of the Infinite. I love to be here. Rama Krishna set us the example."

Turyananda's face glowed with enthusiasm. His hands lay wide open and inert on his lap. If one could overlook the movement of his lips and the fire in his eyes while he was talking, one would at once feel the perfect serenity and poise that characterised him. He embodied the phrase of the poet—"That man is fierce with tranquillity."

Now I asked him the most vital of all my questions. I spoke with a studied slowness in order to make him receive my words without laughing at them again.

"My Lord, what is the message that Rama Krishna has for the West?"

"The West must realize God more. Realization is what Rama Krishna symbolized. Religion is the record of our experience of God, and not a theory of our own belief in God. To the West his message is the same as to the East. Find God. He said to Swami Vivekananda in answer to the question: Can you see God?—'Yes, as I see you, only more intensely.' If Rama Krishna saw and became God, so can you and I. To be religious is to experience and then to believe in God. Belief comes after experience. Belief that precedes experience is not important."

"Yet there is not one belief," I interrupted Him. "Only One God, but so many religions and beliefs."

The holy man fell in line with my thought with perfect ease. He rejoined: "There is only One Truth, but there are so many ways of experiencing Him. And there ought to be as many beliefs as there are experiences of

God. Authentic and important beliefs are but statements of men's realization of their own inherent Godhood. Look, how experiences and statements of them differ in such objective matters as the sun—Men's experiences differ exceedingly. An African's feeling of the sun is quite different from that of a Laplander. They have different stories to tell about the cycles of the sun; the former believes that it shines twelve hours a day, while the latter holds that it shines for six months in a year. Yet it is the same sun. Similarly, with our experience of God. Though we all realize the One Beloved, our ways of stating Him are quite different. Yet all of them verify and magnify His 'thousand-facèdness.' Instead of seeing the same bleak, flat face all the time, we all see many different faces of the One Face of Silence. Does not that make the Lord all the more interesting? You cannot be bored by Him, since by the time you have grown used to seeing one aspect of Him, He has another to reveal to you. He is ever new, for He is for ever the same. As to a growing child its mother seems to display different sides of herself year after year, so does the Mother of the Universe to us. Once, when we are spiritually young, He is our Helper and Sustainer. During our soul's adolescence we find in Him our most intimate friend. In the growing manhood of our spirit, He reveals Himself as a symbol of our experience. And at the end we discover that all those faces that we have looked upon are but facets of our own Immortal Self."

"How can we find that self, my Lord?" I cried out. "So many religious teachers, so many Gurus, create but confusion!" Turyananda paused awhile. He looked at me; then through the small window at the garden without. Slowly he withdrew his gaze and fastened it upon me again. "There are Gurus who have seen the Lord. Find one of those. He will take you into the very nuptial chamber where souls of men are united with the Lord. Such a Guru may come from any caste or religion. He may be a Hindu, a Mohammedan or a Christian, but he alone has the power and the right to take on a disciple. If you have come across one such, go to that

Guru, and he will give you the key to the Chamber of the Bridegroom."

Here someone interrupted us, and the rest of my questions had to remain unasked until the morrow. The next day about four in the afternoon, Turyananda discoursed to me, as he and I walked up and down on the green turf of the Monastery gardens. He appeared quite different, as if he was another man—alert, athletic, noticing things quickly and clearly. Now and then he shouted to a passing white-robed Brahmachari and asked him about the health of certain patients in the hospital. Sometimes he stopped and chatted with the gardener working at a small bush, "about the diseases of certain trees and plants this time of the year," yet all that time—nearly two hours—he kept the thread of our conversation uninterrupted. It was during one of the pauses of his chat with the gardener that he asked me: "You have another inquiry to make. What is it, my son?"

So I put forth another question: "If each man can find God in his own way, then why not through Yoga practices?"

"Yoga practices are singular," he said. "Have you dived deep into Shivananda's pamphlet on that? It is a deep work, that is why it is so short. You must not be deluded by what the Yogi teachers say. For Shivananda is right. If you learn to control your breath, if you increase your powers of concentration, all those things tend to make you strong. Even physical health is affected by them. *Na tasya roga na jara na mrityu praptasya yogagnimayam shariram*—He has no age, disease, nor decay, who has put on the flame-garb of Yoga. That is true. But perpetual youth is no good to you if you cannot find Him, the Ageless, who does not have to be even young.

"Here is another important thing that people intent on Yoga practices overlook. Suppose you concentrate hard on a thought, such as: God is infinite Beauty. In the course of your thinking you will pass over many phases of your own experiences to which you have not paid any attention before. You will pass from your experiences into those of others. Gradually, after a year or two, you will be able to think so hard that your concentration will rise to its highest power. Then your body will begin to behave strangely. Your breathing will cease for many minutes. Your pulse will slacken, and your consciousness of the external world will be reduced nearly to nothing. If you repeat that process a few times more, your concentration will be so intense that occasionally your heart will stop beating for a short while. At last when your object is attained, and you have fathomed the full magnitude of God's Infinite Beauty, lo! incidentally, you have acquired the so-called occult powers of Yoga.

"There is no doubt that while concentrating on the divine, the Rishis, sages, of ancient India, stumbled upon the science of Yoga. It was only an incident of their spiritual life. Alas, unfortunately, later came a race of bastard holy men who did not care much for God. They wanted fireworks. So they prostituted Yoga into a science for acquiring occult power. Rama Krishna warned us against any and every form of spiritual prostitution. If you want power, why don't you become a general, a robber baron, or a highwayman? Why turn Yoga into an end in itself? I have known Yogi teachers who can do many strange things but they cannot find God. These prestidigitators—for that they are and no more—think that they can do something that no one else can. But that is not true. Rama Krishna who was no Yogi, could beat any Yogi at his own game. For in the process of finding God, his heart, breathing, and nervous system suspended work automatically. He acquired this entire bag of Yogi tricks without ever bothering about it.

"Beware, my son! If you search for and find God, all the occult powers will be won unto you. And what is more astonishing than a dwarf's scaling the Himalayas is that once the Beatific Vision has been vouchsafed unto you, you will never be tempted to abuse your powers. Like those great men who, given the freedom of a city never use it, so does one with the privileges of the House of Immortality. The sons of Immortality never stoop to magic or display of power.

"Besides, we are living in an age when men

have neither time nor patience for the thaumaturgy of occultism and Yoga. Men and women nowadays are in a great hurry. Hence they will take short-cuts to the Infinite. In Kali Yuga, this age, the only thing they have to do is to go on wanting the Lord sincerely. If they want Him long, He will reveal Himself to their mortal eyes. There is no doubt of it. He is like the mother-cat who cannot resist the crying call of her kitten very long. Look at Rama Krishna. He found the Mother by simply crying and pleading with Her. Do so yourself and She will at once take down the mask of the sun from Her Face, and reveal to you Her Face of Compassion that is within you. Oh! it is so easy to find God in our time! Look, my child, the sun is setting. It is time to commune with Her. Come into my dwelling and meditate with me. Hari Om, Hari Om."

CHAPTER XVI

LAST IMPRESSION

NOW that I had gathered together as many legends and stories of Rama Krishna as the time at my disposal permitted, I went to pay my last visit to Dakshineswar, the scene of his spiritual struggle and triumphs. I was urged to make a final pilgrimage there by one of the old women who knew the Master and who had told me some interesting tales about him.

So early one morning just when the first flake of sun-gold had fallen on the Ganges, we entered Dakshineswar. The all too familiar picture of age and decay that characterised the place was before us once more. The many domed temples and their decaying gray walls looked uninviting. The gardens that surrounded them were full of weeds. None of the glow and glamor of the old days were discernible anywhere. Instead a steadily augmenting ruin greeted us on every hand. Even the trees under which Rama Krishna meditated were decaying. Unable to bear the sight of so much desolation I asked my aged mentor to take me within the temple. There too I found no relief. The long corridors and the majestic ceilings of the shrine were one vast horror. Plaster and paint were peeling off them; spiders had woven their webs everywhere, and numberless black pigeons had made their nests in every crevice and corner of the ceiling. And far away from the dim inner shrine rose the chant of the ministrant Purohit (priest) like the croon of a hungry ghost.

I started to walk away while I complained bitterly to my ancient guide: "Where has all the joy, Ananda, and glory, Jyoti vanished? Why wears this place such an expression of loneliness?" Her face, as full of wrinkles as an old barn with spider-webs, slowly lit up. Between the innumerable lines of her visage ran a current of expression as clear as crystal waters flowing between the cracks of a black rock.

"Oh, thou dream-seeker," she ejaculated, "his glory was not of this earth. As the music is not in the pipe but in the soul of the player, so was his holiness: it was in him. This place where I have seen hundreds of pilgrims brought on barges, like fortresses of color, is deserted now. Why? Because he is not here. No matter who else—even the queen and her bejeweled women drawing their veils of cerise, amber and pigeon-throated silk against those hard walls white as the shining moon—even they could not bring this place to life. It died the moment Rama Krishna went. Priests, scholars, and Rajahs, they cannot create life. It was his Being that made this place. Even the trees are dying because their roots do not feel his feet treading the ground above them."

"Why did they allow everything—the relics, the simple souvenirs—to die out?" I complained again. "If it had been in Europe they would preserve everything that makes history."

The old crone laughed at me, then unburdened her mind. "Renunciation is what Rama Krishna lived and preached. How can you make history out of Renunciation? Oh, I heard him. I also saw his face. Sometimes he used to go by our cottage after his meditations in Panchabati. Had you seen that face of scorching ecstasy then you would understand: he renounced even his body. He was free. He left nothing bound to himself. He even liberated the room where he lived from the bonds of remembering him. He did not wish to trap souls or places: he was not a fowler of the infinite. He came to free the world."

"If he leaves nothing behind, how are we to know of him?" I asked dialectically.

"But he has made Being," answered the old sybil. "Wherever men and women meditate and live selflessness, there he incarnates. If you wish to make him live again, renounce all and seek God."

"That is all fine talk, Mother," I fretted. "I grant you that a Teacher comes to earth to free us. But there are certain symbols, certain memories that he must leave behind to guide later generations."

"They are not here," she explained. "They are in the Monastery across the river. There men and women meditate as he did—that is his symbol—there they try to live as he did to make God become Man. Is not that the right way to remember him?"

"I suppose I can't make it clear to you," I announced frankly. "I have never seen such a disregard of time and place as in this God-mad country of ours. I am afraid you find me a slave of such illusions as history and geography. I suppose, according to you, even writing and talking about him is useless. They will not bring him to life. Will they?"

"What good are words when you are to tap the Silence of Infinite Compassion?" rang her paradoxical question. "Rama Krishna used to tell a story about himself. Once he went to call on a great initiate, Tailanga. Tailanga lived in Benares. But he observed a strict vow of silence. No one ever heard him speak. Rama Krishna came back from his visit to that silent initiate and told us all about it.

He said: 'Wonderful talks he and I had. Nearly a week we sat beside each other and meditated. A great talker is Tailanga, he unburdens his thoughts with such clear words.' We said to Rama Krishna: 'But he never speaks.' Rama Krishna answered: 'What has that got to do with it?'

"Now you see, my son, what cripples your written and spoken words are. They cannot limp to any place. God fools us with little brains. But Rama Krishna could not be fooled. So He became God."

"Well, Mother, so be it. I shall leave this place of decay and death now, and go across to the monastery whose youth and vigor are more to my taste." And I turned to go.

But she would not let me depart. She said: "Let me bless you, my child. But promise to dine with me to-day."

I promised readily. Pleased with my words, she blessed me. She said: "You loiter here awhile. I will go home and cook. At midday dine in my cottage. Then go across to the monastery. May Rama Krishna load your heart with an agony for God."

Though the conversation of my wise old hostess was most interesting I had to take leave of her. For I had an appointment—in fact my last interview—with the Pundit at the Monastery. That chronicler of Rama Krishna's conversations was coming all the way from the city of Calcutta to see me that afternoon.

As we rowed across the river, the gray temple-towers and the decaying trees of Dakshineswar sank out of sight. And like a banner on the other shore rose the white turret of the Monastery temple. The palms spread their fans in the air on which the afternoon sun shone fiercely. Now we saw ocher-robed figures moving about through green gardens. Turret by turret, roof by roof, the yellow-walled monastery came into full view, and slowly vanished again as we made our boat fast under the stone embankment. Leaping over, I ran up the steps of the Ghaut like a happy squirrel. The life and vigor of the place possessed me at once.

I ran along the wall of the first building, and suddenly beheld the Pundit sitting on the red-tiled terrace waiting for me. After I had seated myself near him, I looked at his bearded face, then said: "My Lord, I leave on the morrow."

He put his fingers through his white beard a few times, then remarked: "Are the Rama Krishna legends that you have gathered tall enough? The legends ought to measure up to His sky-humbling stature."

I said "No, they are not tall. They seem to me quite natural and normal. They are mostly based on reality."

"I do not mean that," he rejoined, bringing his lion-head of a face close to mine. "I mean whatever legend grows up about him will become true."

"I do not understand you." I was puzzled.

"It is simple enough," the Pundit ejaculated with a backward movement of his head. "Look at Christ: even His birth without any earthly father became a reality. Why? Because His Being was so living and so tall that in order to explain Him they had to invent Immaculate Conception. The same was the case with Buddha. He was so divine that they had to invent the same origin for Him, an Immaculate Conception, in order to grasp His essence. All legends become history when their central character is spiritual enough to sustain and give life to them."

"The story of the Immaculate Conception came after Buddha and Christ had become God," I repeated to myself.

The Pundit said, "Yes. The same thing is happening to Rama Krishna. He was so spiritual that in order to explain him, people have to resort to many supernatural explanations. It has been my lot to chronicle only his discourses."

"I wish it were my lot to chronicle the legends," I remarked. "Unfortunately, what people tell me is more or less embedded in facts. Some day I will find those who will tell me of the supernatural higher legends. But, not to change the subject, I should like to ask you, sir, is there any reason why all of you allow the property at Dakshineswar to fall into ruin while you take good care of this place which was built years after Rama Krishna's death?"

"There is no reason," he answered without the slightest delay. "You see how strong the trees look here, how fine the turf, and how healthy the cows, not to speak of the holy men. But this is where Rama Krishna lives. Wherever a few of the servants of Truth dwell, Being precipitates itself. And where there is Being, life grows. All that you see here is a reflection of Being."

"Then that is true of all the disciples and followers of Rama Krishna," I commented.

"Who can deny it?" He expatiated: "When the Master died, we had no place to go to. Now Benares, Kankhal, Bombay, Bangalore, Madras, and dozens of other cities in India, and those that are abroad, have their Rama Krishna Ashrama where men and women gather irrespective of religion and race to live so that a deathless Being is precipitated. It has come faster than I dreamt. But such is the power of the Inner Life that the Holy One lives! We who lived with him know that his Light is steeper than all darkness and will be shed upon the world as long as we can create it through living. It can grow wherever men choose to dwell in purity, holiness and infinite tolerance."

"Why have they not chosen to live in Dakshineswar?" I asked again.

He looked at me with those topaz eyes of his. It was uncomfortable to be gazed at so. Apparently he felt my discomfort, so averting his gaze he said: "I cannot perceive the reason why you should identify the Inner Dakshineswar with the Outer? Rama Krishna lives in the Inner which is in every soul. Wherever that soul goes It goes with him. It is homeless in time as It is houseless in space."

"Then a hundred years from now no pilgrims will flock to that place across where he toiled and triumphed?" I demanded his opinion.

"But men must make pilgrimage to the sanctities within them. Why should they go to a place without? I hope no one will cheapen and exploit that place, Dakshineswar. Rama Krishna has left nothing there that can in the slightest serve as a pretext for starting a new cult with its horrors of priest-craft and terrors of commercialism."

"Then you too are against history?" I criticised him.

The Pundit said: "Rama Krishna was a galloping torch that came to earth to light other torches—souls of men and women—so that each one of them would become God. He wanted every one of us to find not a religion, but to be Religion. He set us that example."

"No priest, no Rabbi, no Padre—it is very difficult for an average man to give up all that to find God within himself."

To that remark of mine he answered: "But those mendicants, priests, do not make Religion. It is men and women who long for God and make Him. Rama Krishna said so. And it is true of our time. This is a new age. It is the high noon of freedom and equality. Men are not surrendering their uniqueness of soul and intelligence to other men. On the contrary they are asserting with tumultuous pride that each one of them is a son of God. If that is so in the outer life of man, how much more so must it be in the inner realm. Men do not wish to bend the knee any more to Avataras and Masters. They themselves would be the Avataras. Every soul is golden-wombed. It must give birth to God, the Timeless. That you cannot bring about by preserving Dakshineswar, Kapilavastu and Bethlehem. What have places or creeds to do with the purity of that Being that men pour into this world through the realisation of their Inner Life? Wherever men and women flock to kindle and quicken their souls, there incarnates the Truth of Rama Krishna."

A strange light came into the Pundit's eyes. It was like tears—so full and so tangible.

By now the afternoon was far spent. The opposite shore—Dakshineswar—sank into deepening purple dusk. The boats loosed their sails that had been gleaming like sunset clouds of amber, amethyst, and rose. They slowly drifted shorewards, and in a few minutes about a dozen of them were moored at the Monastery Ghaut. Then their half-naked boatmen, like brown Tritons, trooped up the steps with baskets of fruits, flowers, and rice to offer to the monks as Dakshina, presents. They left their offering at the door of a hut, then walked towards the inner shrine in order to attend Arati.

Swiftly the day was passing into the night. Silence like a black panther began to prowl about us. We felt beset with sanctities. The Pundit said to me: "Do you meditate, or, do you go hence now?"

"I go, my Lord," I answered, "to begin my story. This evening I do not meditate." He blessed me. Then added: "I must go and pray. May your soul pour compassion upon all. Farewell!"

In a minute he was gone. As I slowly went down the steps of the Ghaut, the sound of a gong smote the air. I listened as I sat still on my boat. Soon came the chant of many voices. I knew what they were saying. So I chanted!

"O thou River of miracles that is within me, pour the healing waters of compassion on the wounded body of Man and make him whole."

Now that I had hymned Silence we rowed our boat towards Calcutta. As we drifted down the tide my imagination wandered back to the inner shrine of the Monastery. I imagined myself sitting within, still attending Arati. With my mind's eyes I saw those innumerable lamps lift their fragrant flames toward the image of Rama Krishna on the altar. The yellow-robed monk waved lit candles before it, while I sat outside and sang again and again "O River of Miracles . . ."

By the time we had reached the Calcutta side of the Ganges it was starry night. The blue-black sky vaulted above, haughty with aloofness, and the stars hung so low that they seemed intimate. Far off in the west the lamps of the various monastery buildings and of the boats below were being lighted one by one.

What did it all mean? Shall I ever be able to tell even a fraction of the joy and peace that was vouchsafed me by those ocher-robed monks? Is it possible that men can live such a vivid life that it becomes a galloping torch of Truth which the material darkness of our time cannot obscure? What had I witnessed? Did I dream these days over there in the monastery? Or, did I truly live as I had never lived before?

Cogitating in the above manner I reached home. Can words translate for the reader Tat, That, which burns in the eyes of those monks across the river? Can anything in any language render the militant peace of the Soul that men have won for themselves and for the world they live in? And is there anywhere in any age one single metaphor or a symbol which adequately conveys the meaning of That? Holiness alone can explain Holiness. And only in so far as we ourselves become Sons of Immortality shall we be able to understand those Sons of God who have sought to help mankind.